THE SPY WHO
COULDN'T SPELL

THE SPY WHO
COULDN'T SPELL

A DYSLEXIC TRAITOR, AN UNBREAKABLE CODE,
AND THE FBI'S HUNT FOR AMERICA'S STOLEN SECRETS

YUDHIJIT BHATTACHARJEE

NEW AMERICAN LIBRARY
New York

NEW AMERICAN LIBRARY
Published by Berkley
An imprint of Penguin Random House LLC
375 Hudson Street, New York, New York 10014

Copyright © 2016 by Yudhijit Bhattacharjee

Library of Congress Cataloging-in-Publication Data
Names: Bhattacharjee, Yudhijit, author.
Title: The spy who couldn't spell: a dyslexic traitor, an unbreakable code,
and the FBI's hunt for America's stolen secrets/Yudhijit Bhattacharjee.
Description: New York, NY: New American Library, 2016.
Identifiers: LCCN 2016012584 (print) I LCCN 2016024121 (ebook) I ISBN 9781592409006
(hardback) I ISBN 9780698404090 (ebook)
Subjects: LCSH: Regan, Brian, 1962– I Spies—United States—Biography. I Espionage,
American—History—21st century. I Dyslexics—United States—Biography. I Intelligence
service—United States—History—21st century. I United States. National Reconnaissance
Office I United States. Federal Bureau of Investigation. I BISAC: TRUE CRIME/Espionage. I
HISTORY/Modern/21st Century. I POLITICAL SCIENCE/
Political Freedom & Security/Intelligence.
Classification: LCC JK468.I6 B48 2016 (print) I LCC JK468.I6 (ebook) I
DDC 364.1/31 [B]—dc23
LC record available at https://lccn.loc.gov/2016012584

First Edition: November 2016

Printed in the United States of America
1   3   5   7   9   10   8   6   4   2

Jacket design by Colleen Reinhart
Book design by Kelly Lipovich

*To Jen, my companion for life,
and to Victor and Zoe, who bring joy to our hearts*

CONTENTS

THE SPY WHO
COULDN'T SPELL

PRELUDE

The classrooms and hallways of Farmingdale High in Long Island were deserted on the morning of Saturday, August 19, 2001, when a van pulled into the school's parking lot. After turning off the engine, the driver of the vehicle—a tall man in his late thirties—stepped out into the warm summer sun. He cast a sweeping gaze upon the buildings and grounds of the institution he'd graduated from two decades earlier.

Whatever nostalgia he might have felt for his old school was tinged with bitterness. For it was here that he had suffered some of life's early humiliations: taunted by classmates for his apparent dim-wittedness; held in low esteem by his teachers. If they remembered him at all, they would remember him as the boy who had difficulty reading, the boy who was so bad at spelling. His bearish frame might have sheltered him from physical bullying in his last years of school, but combined with his severe dyslexia and his social awkwardness, it had also cemented his image as a dolt.

That image had stuck with him, despite a successful career in U.S. intelligence and a top secret security clearance that gave him access to some of the country's most valued secrets. Being underestimated—by family, classmates, and colleagues—had been the theme of his life, a curse he had borne silently since childhood. But for the mission he had now embarked upon, it was a blessing. None of his colleagues or managers in the intelligence community could have imagined that he of all people—so lacking in flamboyance as to be the antithesis of James Bond—was capable of masterminding such a cunning espionage conspiracy.

From the parking lot, he walked to the edge of the school grounds. Squeezing through a hole in the barbed-wire fence next to the handball courts, he stepped into a wooded area that separated the Southern State Parkway from the school perimeter. After walking a few yards, he stopped by a tree and dug a hole in the ground. He took a laminated phone list out of his pocket and buried it there before walking back through the fence to his van, confident that nobody had seen him.

He'd already pulled off the biggest heist of classified information in the annals of American espionage. In just a few days, he hoped to execute the final step of a meticulous plan to exchange those secrets for millions of dollars. If he succeeded, he would have enough money to pay off his brothers' and sisters' mortgages, settle his personal debts, and secure his children's financial future.

With fortune, he imagined, respect would follow. Those who had known him would no longer doubt his intelligence. Once and for all, he would shake the mantle of stupid.

CHAPTER 1

THE TIP

On the morning of the first Monday in December 2000, FBI special agent Steven Carr hurried out of his cubicle at the bureau's Washington, D.C., field office and bounded down two flights of stairs to pick up a package that had just arrived by FedEx from FBI New York. Carr was thirty-eight years old, of medium build, with blue eyes and a handsome face. He was thoughtful and intense, meticulous in his work, driven by a sense of patriotic duty inherited from his father, who served in World War II, and his maternal and paternal grandfathers, who both fought in World War I. Because of his aptitude for deduction and his intellectual doggedness, he'd been assigned to counterintelligence within a year after coming to the FBI in 1995. In his time at the bureau—all of it spent in the nation's capital—he had played a supporting role in a series of high-profile espionage cases, helping to investigate spies such as Jim Nicholson, the flamboyant CIA agent who sold U.S. secrets to the Russians.

But like most agents starting out in their careers, Carr was keen to lead a high-stakes investigation himself. A devout Catholic, Carr would sometimes bow his head in church and say a silent prayer requesting the divine's help in landing a good case. That's why he had responded with such alacrity when his squad supervisor, Lydia Jechorek, had asked him to pick up the package that morning. "Whatever it is, it's yours," she had said.

Carr raced back to his desk and laid out the contents of the package in front of him: a sheaf of papers running into a few dozen pages. They were from three envelopes that had been handed to FBI New York by a confidential informant at the Libyan consulate in New York. The envelopes had been individually mailed to the consulate by an unknown sender.

Breathlessly, Carr thumbed through the sheets. Based on directions sent from New York, he was able to sort the papers into three sets corresponding to the three envelopes. All three had an identical cover sheet, at the top of which was a warning in all caps. "THIS LETTER CONTAINS SENSITIVE INFORMATION." Below, it read, in part:

"This letter is confidential and directed to your President or Intelligence Chief. Please pass this letter via diplomatic pouch and do not discuss the existence of this letter in your offices or homes or via any electronic means. If you do not follow these instructions the existence of this letter and its contents may be detected and collected by U.S. intelligence agencies."

In the first envelope was a four-page letter with 149 lines of typed text consisting of alphabetical characters and numbers. The second envelope included instructions on how to decode the letter. The third envelope included two sets of code sheets. One set contained a list of ciphers. The other, running to six pages, listed dozens of words along with their encoded abbreviations: a system commonly known as brevity codes. Together, the two sets were meant to serve as the key for the decryption.

Carr flipped through the letter, skimming the alphanumeric sequence. It looked like gibberish, like text you might get if you left a curious monkey in front of a keyboard. There was no way to make sense of it without the code sheets and the decoding instructions. By mailing the three separately, the sender had sought to secure the communication against the possibility that one envelope might get intercepted by a U.S. intelligence agency. Carr saw that the sender had included a message in typed plaintext in each envelope, informing the consulate of the other two envelopes in the mail and instructing the receiver of the message to place a car ad in the *Washington Post* if any of the other envelopes failed to arrive. The sender had not anticipated that all three envelopes could fall into the FBI's hands.

FBI New York had already decoded a few lines of the letter. Carr's pulse quickened further as he read the deciphered text.

"I am a Middle East North African analyst for the Central Intelligence Agency. I am willing to commit espionage against the U.S. by providing your country with highly classified information. I have a top secret clearance and have access to documents of all of the U.S. intelligence agencies, National Security Agency (NSA), Defense Intelligence Agency (DIA), Central Command (CENTCOM) as well as smaller agencies."

To prove that this wasn't a bluff, the sender had included in all three envelopes an identical set of government documents, twenty-three pages in all, some marked "CLASSIFIED SECRET," some

"CLASSIFIED TOP SECRET." Most of them were aerial images taken by U.S. spy satellites showing military sites in the Middle East and other parts of the world: air defense systems, weapons depots, munitions factories, underground bunkers. Some of the documents were intelligence reports about regimes and militaries in the Middle East. It was evident from the markings on these images and reports that they had been printed after being downloaded from Intelink, a classified network of servers that constituted the intelligence community's Internet.

There were some additional documents. One was a monthly newsletter of the CIA, circulated internally among agency employees. Another was the table of contents of the *Joint Tactical Exploitation of National Systems*, a classified manual to help the U.S. war fighter take advantage of the country's reconnaissance satellites and other intelligence-gathering technologies. The manual had been compromised before by another spy—an NSA cryptologist named David Sheldon Boone, who had sold it to the Soviet Union a decade earlier. In the years since, as the United States' reconnaissance capabilities had evolved, the manual had been updated a number of times. The table of contents the sender had included in the package was from the manual's most recent version. It would be valuable even to an adversary already in possession of the *JTENS* that Boone had given away.

Also among the documents were aerial photographs of Gaddhafi's yacht in the Mediterranean Sea. They had been taken from a low-flying aircraft deployed not by the United States but by a foreign intelligence service. How the sender of the package could have acquired them was unclear.

Carr studied the pages in stunned silence, oblivious to the

comings and goings of colleagues around him. He had never seen anything like this before. Since joining the squad, he had followed up on dozens of letters tipping the FBI off to potential espionage. Most came from anonymous sources at U.S. intelligence agencies accusing a coworker or colleague of being a spy. Rarely did such "point and pin" letters lead to the discovery of a real threat: more often than not, they turned out to be a case of erroneous judgment by the tipster or a case of bitter workplace jealousy.

What Carr had in front of him seemed anything but a false alarm. The sender of the envelopes was no doubt a bona fide member of the U.S. intelligence community, with access to top secret documents, intent on establishing a clandestine relationship with a foreign intelligence service. The person had, in fact, already committed espionage by giving classified information to an enemy country. Carr might as well have been looking at a warning sign for a national security threat flashing in neon red.

Despite his excitement, Carr filed the sheets neatly into a binder before stepping into his supervisor's office. "Lydia," he said, sliding the binder across her desk. "You have to look at this."

Jechorek leafed through the pages. A short-haired, bespectacled woman in her early fifties, she had a quiet manner that belied a tough-as-nails personality. She had gotten hooked to law enforcement early in life, joining her father—a police officer—on surveillance runs and drawing sketches of murder suspects while still a sophomore in high school. Now a veteran of counterintelligence, Jechorek was best known for having led the FBI's investigation of Jonathan Pollard, the spy who was caught selling U.S. secrets to Israel in the eighties.

Carr explained to her why FBI New York had couriered the pages to Washington. In the portion of the coded letter that agents in New York had deciphered, they had found an e-mail address the sender wanted to use for further communication. With special permission from the U.S. attorney general, the nation's top law enforcement official, the agents asked the e-mail service provider to let them pry into the account: jacobscall@mail.com.

They discovered that the account had been created four months earlier, on August 3, using Internet access from a public library in Prince George's County, Maryland. In the account registration, the user had identified himself as "Steven Jacobs," having a residential address in Alexandria, Virginia. The account had been accessed half a dozen times from public libraries around Washington, D.C. There were no e-mails in the account except for test messages the person had sent to himself, and a reply from the Fraud Bureau in response to an inquiry he had made about an online company that sold fake IDs. From the accesses, the New York agents were certain that the individual lived somewhere in the greater Washington, D.C., metropolitan area.

"What are we going to do?" Jechorek asked, the urgency in her tone mirroring Carr's. It was imperative that the FBI find this person as quickly as possible. Perhaps it was already too late.

Carr showed her a matrix of clues he'd built from his gleaning of the pages. The system of brevity codes the sender had used—along with the concern for operational security—pointed to somebody with a military background. That surmise was founded on Carr's own experience in the military: before coming to the FBI, he had spent eleven years in the U.S. Army and the National Guard, where he had used brevity codes in training exercises to communicate with fellow troops. In Carr's estimation, the sender of the envelopes likely had a more sophisticated knowledge of cryptology than just brevity codes. He had a top secret security clearance, which was marginally helpful, since it reduced the potential suspect pool from the few hundred thousand workers in the U.S. intelligence community who have a secret security clearance to a more limited population, on the order of tens of thousands, with the higher level of clearance. He also had access to Intelink. And he was likely married, with children, as evidenced by a line in the letter stating, "If I commit espionage, I will be putting myself and family at great risk."

There was one other thing: the man was a terrible speller.

Scanning the six pages of brevity codes, Carr spotted one misspelled word after another. The sender had evidently put this codebook together by first printing out the typed letter in plaintext, then cutting out individual words and pasting them alongside abbreviations that he'd printed out separately on other sheets. Carr could deduce that because the words didn't line up perfectly with the individual abbreviations. But the disorderliness in alignment was hardly as glaring as the misspellings.

AP: Anonmus
NH: Alligations
GR: Reveil
16: Precausion
CN: Negotianalable
DZ: Airbourn
KJ: Assocation
MY: Netralize
YF: Confrimed

The list went on and on. Here was a person who had gone to great lengths to accomplish operational security but failed to run a basic spell-check.

For the moment, though, Carr was focused on another set of clues: the locations of the public libraries the sender had accessed the jacobscall e-mail account from. He'd marked them with pins on a large map of the Washington, D.C., metropolitan area. The pins were clustered in and around the towns of Bowie and Crofton in Maryland. The intelligence agency in closest proximity was the National Security Agency.

Located in Fort Meade, Maryland, the NSA has thousands of military employees, many with a background in cryptology, many with homes in the towns of Bowie and Crofton. Carr's hunch was that the traitor was likely from within the NSA's ranks, even though he'd introduced himself as a CIA analyst. That line—and the CIA newsletter in the materials he had sent—was possibly a red herring.

"We need to call Mac," Carr said.

Jechorek picked up the phone and dialed Robert McCaslin, the head of counterintelligence at the NSA.

"Hello," McCaslin answered. An old-timer in counterintelligence circles, he spoke with the deep, authoritative voice of someone who was not used to being challenged.

"I'd like to come over to talk to you about an important matter," Jechorek said.

"I'm really busy right now," he replied. "The earliest we can do it is tomorrow."

Jechorek, who didn't know McCaslin too well, was reluctant to press him further.

She hung up.

"What did he say?" Carr asked her.

"He says he can't see us until tomorrow."

"Tomorrow? You've got to call him back."

Jechorek studied the binder for a few moments. Then she reached for the phone and punched "redial."

"Hi, Lydia," McCaslin answered tersely.

"We are coming to see you right now," Jechorek said. Her tone was polite but firm.

McCaslin knew at once that this couldn't wait.

"OK, we'll clear our schedule," he said.

Carr and Jechorek sped along Interstate 295, leaving behind the bustle of Washington, D.C. Most of the trees along the highway were shorn of leaves, fall having blended into winter. The two agents took the exit for the NSA's sprawling annex in Elkridge, a few miles from the Baltimore airport. Less than an hour after Jechorek's phone call to McCaslin, the agents were in his office.

McCaslin browsed the pages with rising alarm, listening to Carr explain why he thought the mailer of the letter could be at the NSA. No counterintelligence officer wants to hear that a spy could be operating within the ranks of his own agency. But looking at the indicators that Carr had derived from his preliminary analysis, McCaslin had to confront the possibility.

There was an additional reason to trust Carr's hunch. Over the summer, NSA's management had announced that it would be laying off some two thousand agency employees, nearly a tenth of its workforce. The announcement came in the wake of a massive computer failure that froze the NSA's internal communications, sparking criticism from lawmakers that the agency had grown into a gigantic, inefficient bureaucracy. McCaslin had to wonder if one of the employees facing retrenchment had decided to walk down the dark path of treason.

The immediate help that Carr and Jechorek wanted from McCaslin was a decryption of the entire letter. Carr had already faxed a copy of it to the FBI's own cryptanalysts. To be doubly sure, he wanted the NSA to work on it in parallel. McCaslin got two of his agency's code breakers on the job right away.

A cryptanalyst's job is to crack coded messages in the absence of a key. In the case of the letter, since the codebook and decoding instructions were on hand, breaking out the 149 lines of coded text didn't involve any puzzle solving. Even so, FBI and NSA cryptanalysts found the task maddeningly complex. Without the key, they would have found it practically impossible to decrypt the letter.

The writer of the letter had used an archaic encryption system dating back to the sixteenth century, which was a heyday for the development of secret writing. It was developed by an Italian cryptographer named Giovan Battista Bellaso, who was a secretary to a cardinal in Camerino and needed to communicate in code with his master when the cardinal was away in Rome. Bellaso's cryptological was innovation, which he described in the 1553 booklet *La Cifra del Sig. Giovan Battista Bel[l]aso*, was erroneously attributed to the sixteenth-century French diplomat and author Blaise de Vigenère, and has popularly come to be known as the Vigenère cipher.

Codes and ciphers, though the terms are used interchangeably, are not quite the same thing. A code is a word or phrase or number that means something else: if you and I decided in advance that the word "red" means "danger" and the word "lotus" stands for "tonight," the phrase "red lotus" would be code for "danger tonight." By contrast, a cipher is a sequence of steps to convert a letter or digit into another symbol that, by itself, doesn't convey any meaning. So, if we decided on a cipher that involves converting letters into numbers that correspond to the positions of the letters in the alphabet, with a dot after each letter and a star between words, "Danger tonight" would be enciphered as 4.1.14.7.5.18*20.15.14. 9.7.8.20. Needless to say, this kind of cipher wouldn't be very secure.

The Vigenère cipher, however, remained unbroken for nearly three centuries, until a German infantry officer named Friedrich Kasiski published a method for systematically attempting to crack it. The cipher's strength lay in its use of multiple alphabets. Unlike the cipher described previously, in which the same reference set of symbols—the English alphabet, sequenced A to Z, where A is 1 and Z is 26—is used for enciphering each letter in the message, the Vigenère cipher uses a different reference set for different letters.

Take the same message: "Danger tonight." To encipher it using the simplest form of the Vigenère method, we would first create what's known as a Vigenère table, consisting of rows of the English alphabet written out in sequence, wherein every successive row is shifted one letter forward. So, the first row starts with A and ends with Z, the second row starts B, C, D . . . and ends with A, and so on, until the twenty-sixth row, which starts Z, A, B, C . . . and ends with Y.

We end up with a matrix of letters, 26 by 26. If we index both the columns and rows A–Z, here's what the matrix would look like:

```
  A B C D E F G H I J K L M N O P Q R S T U V W X Y Z
A A B C D E F G H I J K L M N O P Q R S T U V W X Y Z
B B C D E F G H I J K L M N O P Q R S T U V W X Y Z A
C C D E F G H I J K L M N O P Q R S T U V W X Y Z A B
D D E F G H I J K L M N O P Q R S T U V W X Y Z A B C
E E F G H I J K L M N O P Q R S T U V W X Y Z A B C D
F F G H I J K L M N O P Q R S T U V W X Y Z A B C D E
G G H I J K L M N O P Q R S T U V W X Y Z A B C D E F
H H I J K L M N O P Q R S T U V W X Y Z A B C D E F G
I I J K L M N O P Q R S T U V W X Y Z A B C D E F G H
J J K L M N O P Q R S T U V W X Y Z A B C D E F G H I
K K L M N O P Q R S T U V W X Y Z A B C D E F G H I J
L L M N O P Q R S T U V W X Y Z A B C D E F G H I J K
M M N O P Q R S T U V W X Y Z A B C D E F G H I J K L
N N O P Q R S T U V W X Y Z A B C D E F G H I J K L M
O O P Q R S T U V W X Y Z A B C D E F G H I J K L M N
P P Q R S T U V W X Y Z A B C D E F G H I J K L M N O
Q Q R S T U V W X Y Z A B C D E F G H I J K L M N O P
R R S T U V W X Y Z A B C D E F G H I J K L M N O P Q
S S T U V W X Y Z A B C D E F G H I J K L M N O P Q R
T T U V W X Y Z A B C D E F G H I J K L M N O P Q R S
U U V W X Y Z A B C D E F G H I J K L M N O P Q R S T
V V W X Y Z A B C D E F G H I J K L M N O P Q R S T U
W W X Y Z A B C D E F G H I J K L M N O P Q R S T U V
X X Y Z A B C D E F G H I J K L M N O P Q R S T U V W
Y Y Z A B C D E F G H I J K L M N O P Q R S T U V W X
Z Z A B C D E F G H I J K L M N O P Q R S T U V W X Y
```

What the matrix represents is twenty-six sets of alphabets, the first starting with *A*, the twenty-sixth starting with *Z*. The

Vigenère cipher uses this table in combination with another security feature: a key. This is a word or a phrase—agreed upon in advance between the sender and receiver of the message—that determines which particular alphabetic set is to be used as the reference for enciphering a particular letter in the message. Here's how.

Let's say our key is the word "BOOK." To encipher our message, "DANGERTONIGHT," line up the key below the plaintext, letter for letter, repeating the key as many times as necessary:

```
Plaintext: DANGERTONIGHT
      Key: BOOKBOOKBOOKB
```

To encipher the letter *D*, find the row of alphabets on the table that starts with the first letter of the key, which is *B*. Where this row meets the column under *D* gives us the enciphered letter: *E*. To encipher the next letter in the message, we go to the row of alphabets starting with the second letter of the key, and we get the enciphered letter *O*. Following that procedure for the entire length of the message, we get a string of ciphertext that reads: "EOBQFFHYOWURU."

The letter sent to the embassy was enciphered using the same principle of "polyalphabetic substitution," but instead of a standard Vigenère table as the reference, the writer had used seventy-one alphabetic sets. Some of them included digits in addition to letters. He'd numbered the pages of the letter confusingly—perhaps to add another layer of security or perhaps erroneously—marking the sixth page as page 1, the fourth as page 2, and so on.

Arranging the pages in the right order, the cryptanalysts had to number the lines of coded text 1 through 149 and follow a complicated set of instructions to pick out the alphabetic set the writer had designated for each line. When this tedious task was done, the analysts had before them several pages of brevity codes strung together: JX KK 16 LX 35 . . .

The next step was to consult the codebook and substitute each of the brevity codes for the word it represented. The writer had chosen not to use codes for certain words, such as "CIA" and "espionage." These words were enciphered in their entirety—letter for letter—and flagged within the coded text with a star or another symbol. This, too, the cryptanalysts realized, was a security measure. If the codebook ended up in the wrong hands—the writer had thought—words like "espionage" would raise an immediate alarm.

The FBI and the NSA spent the next two days breaking out the letter. When Carr read the decoded text in full, it took his breath away. Continuing on from the introductory paragraphs, the letter read:

I have been in the CIA for over 20 years and will be retiring in two years. I feel that I deserve more than the small pension I will receive for all the years of service at the CIA.

In that vein of entitlement, it went on:

Considering the risk I am about to take I will require a minimum payment of thirteen million U.S. dollars wire transferred in Swiss francs, the exact amount, before I will risk my life. There are many people from movie stars to athletes in the U.S. who are receiving tens of millions of dollars a year for their trivial contributions. If I am going to risk my life and the future of my family, I am going to get paid a fair price. The information I am offering will compromise U.S. intelligence systems worth hundreds of billions of dollars. Thirteen million is a small price to pay for what you will receive.

The letter proceeded to list the kinds of information that this money would buy, starting with the *JTENS* manual, whose table of contents the spy had included in the documents intended to prove access.

This top-secret document will provide you with highly secretive information on U.S. satellites, airborne and ground intelligence systems. . . . I will also provide you with a list of the actual locations and orbits of all of the U.S. spy satellites, which can be loaded into any standard software package. This top-secret information will provide your country with the scheduled times U.S. satellites will be overhead and collecting against your country and when these systems are out of range of your country.

The text that followed laid out in painstaking detail how the transaction was to be conducted. First, to prove to the spy that the letter had been read by its intended recipient, the Libyan intelligence service was to make a small change to the country's United Nations home page—"switch one word for another, add a comma or change some numbers."

Next, the spy wanted the client country to place an ad for a used car in the classified section of the *Washington Post*. It was to say:

FORD 93 Taurus GL
Silver, loaded, sunroof
95K miles $17,000 / OBO (Or best offer)

None of the car's details was significant. Rather, the key information the ad was to convey was an 800 number the spy had instructed Libyan intelligence to set up.

"I need you to place a representative in the USA or activate someone who is currently in the U.S. who you can trust and I can contact," the letter said, suggesting that the intelligence service select a "loyal" Libyan student attending a U.S. college or some other trusted individual who couldn't be easily linked to the Libyan government. "Have this person establish a 1-800 phone number in his home. He does not need to know who I am or how I got this phone number. If he is caught, he cannot compromise the entire operation."

For an added layer of security—as if there weren't enough layers already—the ad wasn't supposed to list the 800 number; instead, it was to provide a phone number derived from reversing the last seven digits of the 800 number. "If 1-800-456-2738 was the number, change it to 1-800-837-2654, then drop the 1-800 and add 703. I will know to drop the 703 when I use the number."

The spy would keep an eye out for the ad, and once it was published, he would call the 800 number and ask to speak with "John Stevens." The Libyan representative answering the call would then provide a mailing address where the spy would mail instructions to decode a bank account number that he would send under separate cover. After confirming that a sum of Swiss francs equivalent to $13 million had been transferred into the account, the spy would FedEx the promised package of top secret information to the same mailing address. Going forward, the spy would mail a new package of information every three months, which Libyan intelligence could review and pay for. "I expect a minimum of three million dollars for each shipment of information that is good, and five million for information that is considered extremely important to your government," the letter said.

The instructions went beyond the mechanics of the transaction: there was also helpful advice on how the Libyans could smuggle the purchased information out of the United States. The spy's recommendation was to follow a series of steps as elaborate as those he'd spelled out for establishing contact: have somebody pick up the package from where it had been mailed, drive it to New York, and hide it in a suitcase in the closet of a rented hotel room. Leave the room key in an envelope at the front desk. Finally, have somebody from the Libyan mission at the United Nations retrieve the package from the hotel room and send it out of the country via diplomatic pouch, which by protocol is shielded from scrutiny.

Whoever had written the letter was evidently familiar with the tradecraft of espionage, perhaps even enamored of it. There was also a discernible arrogance in the message. The repetitious warnings about how to keep the operation secure, a strident declaration—early in the letter—that the price was nonnegotiable, the gratuitous counseling on how to beat U.S. counterintelligence: all were signals of the spy thinking that he knew best—not just what was good for him but also what was good for the Libyans. He also seemed to want to draw attention to how clever he was, obliquely explaining in the letter why he had chosen to market information to Libya rather than the United States' traditional rival, Russia.

"The reason I am going to remain anonymous is that most spies are caught because when someone defects to the west, they take with them the names of all the western spies they know of," he wrote. "This is why no one would attempt to spy for the Russians today. There are too many Russians turning over their agents to the U.S. Since I do not want to be caught, and you should not want me to be caught, I will remain anonymous."

If the complexity of the spy's plan was anything to go by, lifting that veil of anonymity was going to be a daunting task. It was exactly the kind of task that Steve Carr had been waiting for since he came to the FBI.

Many of the FBI's twelve thousand agents are men and women who have dreamed of working at the bureau since they were kids. As a boy, Carr nurtured a different dream: he wanted to become a pilot. Growing up in Gaithersburg, Maryland, he was surrounded by relatives and family friends who had served in the military. His father's father, who had fought as an infantryman in World War I, was buried at Arlington National Cemetery. Carr would badger his maternal grandfather, another World War I veteran, to narrate his battlefield experiences. A reluctant storyteller, the old man would sometimes oblige his grandson, recounting how he fought through the haze of mustard gas and how the French machine gun he used got jammed in the heat of battle, compelling him to duck and grab his pistol.

Fascinated by these accounts, Carr, eight years old at the time, enacted warlike heroics in his backyard with toy army men, throwing rocks at them and sliding them along zip lines. He would draw pictures of helicopters and planes and tell relatives and friends he was "a hundred percent certain" that he wanted to join the army when he grew up. Camping with his family on Assateague Island off the coast of Maryland, he spent hours sitting on top of a model submarine at a playground near the campsite, peering through its red periscope and pretending to launch torpedoes at imaginary

U-boats gliding through the blue waters of the Atlantic. His interest in military history would grow into a passion in his adulthood, leading him to always keep a metal detector in his car while driving up and down the East Coast, so that he could hunt for and dig up Civil War relics.

By ten, Carr was hooked on flight, craning his neck to squint at the sky every time an airplane flew overhead. In seventh grade, he got into trouble at school. It angered him to see a group of classmates ganging up on a fellow student who had a severe intellectual disability. When they stole the student's food and teased him, Carr protested: more precisely, he expressed his disapproval by hitting one of the bullies in the head with a paper-clip slingshot. The principal didn't take kindly to Carr's method of protest. Combined with reports of other behavioral problems and a string of bad grades, the incident helped convince his parents that military school—which Carr had shown an interest in—would be a better place for him.

Carr to the Fishburne Military School in Virginia, thrived. After college, in the late eighties, he became a helicopter pilot in the military. Although it was an exciting stint, the job didn't quite match up to Carr's dream of flying in combat, since the United States wasn't engaged in any major conflicts overseas and he wasn't deployed abroad. After five years, he decided he wanted to do something else. He left active duty to work for his father's electrical contracting business and joined the Maryland National Guard.

One summer day in 1994, he was lounging on Bethany Beach with his wife when he spotted an old friend he had lost touch with years ago. The friend, an FBI agent, suggested that Carr give the bureau a try. Carr, who was not keen to stay tethered to the family business, decided it was a good idea. He would come to see the chance meeting as divine providence. "God was taking this cosmic baseball bat and hitting me over the head to apply," he told colleagues after joining the bureau.

The remark reflected the kind of person Carr was: a firm believer in the idea that God was the master of his destiny. This belief was the bedrock of Carr's outlook on life, driving his desire to serve his fellow men and women in any capacity he could. On nights and weekends, he and his wife, Michelle, provided premarital counseling to couples on behalf of his church. Serving the country—first as a military pilot and then as an FBI agent—was to Carr a way of serving God. It was as much a spiritual calling as it was a career choice. And so it was that through the last weeks of 2000, as winter's chill deepened over Washington, D.C., Carr's every waking hour became consumed by a zealous hunt for the spy who couldn't spell.

Even though Carr's hunch had pointed him to the NSA, there were no grounds to eliminate other intelligence agencies as possibilities. The day after his visit to the NSA, Carr went over to Langley, Virginia, to brief the CIA.

Counterintelligence officials there couldn't imagine a career CIA analyst making so many spelling errors. It wasn't just a conceited opinion, though. Like Carr, they thought the spy's self-description as a CIA analyst was a possible red herring, and that, too, an elaborate one. The CIA newsletter that the spy had included in the bona fides even listed an agency employee whose last name was Jacobs, matching the last name that the spy had used when opening the jacobscall e-mail account. Based on a host of factors, that person was quickly ruled out as a suspect. The Alexandria address the spy had provided to register the e-mail account was the home of a woman whose last name was also Jacobs. The spy had clearly put some thought into creating the fake identity.

Nonetheless, it was still possible that the spy was from within the CIA's ranks, even if he wasn't a Middle Eastern–North African analyst. And so the CIA joined the search, along with the NSA.

On December 13, more than a week after he'd seen the coded letter, Carr drove out to the National Reconnaissance Office in Chantilly, Virginia. Responsible for managing the nation's spy satellites, the NRO was one of the United States' most secretive organizations. For three decades after it was founded, most Americans didn't even know that it existed. Despite an annual budget of several billion dollars, the shroud of secrecy surrounding the NRO stayed intact well after its existence was made public in 1993. The organization's relative obscurity—even to intelligence insiders—was why Carr hadn't thought of it right away.

But over the course of the week, he had come to realize that the spy could well be a current or former employee of the NRO. Like the NSA, the NRO is heavily staffed by members of the U.S. military. It fitted with Carr's hypothesis about the traitor being a military man. Another reason was that the jacobscall e-mail address had been accessed not just from libraries in Bowie and Crofton, but also on one occasion from the Tysons-Pimmit Regional Library in Falls Church, Virginia, within fifteen miles of the NRO's headquarters in Chantilly. It was plausible, Carr thought, that the spy lived close to the NSA and worked at the NRO.

As Carr familiarized himself with the NRO's mission and operations, he could see the clues in the spy's letter and bona fides that pointed in the direction of that agency. A lot of the secrets the spy was offering—aerial imagery and signals intelligence—constituted exactly the kind of information that the NRO's satellites collected on their clandestine orbits around the Earth. Since the NSA, the CIA, and several other agencies access and use these intelligence products routinely, one couldn't link those secrets exclusively to the NRO. Yet other details in the letter—such as the offer to provide orbits, locations, and schedules of satellites—indicated a familiarity with reconnaissance from space.

The NRO launched an internal investigation to identify potential suspects in its employee pool. The CIA and the NSA had already begun searching within their ranks. In the meantime, investigators visited the different libraries the spy had accessed the jacobscall e-mail account from, in hopes of finding records of who might have been sitting at the libraries' public computers at those times. Much to the FBI's dismay—and to the relief of privacy advocates—the library administrations didn't keep such records. At the Tysons-Pimmit Regional Library, for instance, patrons waiting to use the Internet stations had to write their names on a list that was tossed at the end of the day.

The e-mail account, however, remained pivotal to the investigation. The FBI asked Mail.com if agents could keep tabs on the jacobscall address, and engineers at the company wrote a special program for the e-mail account. It was designed to send an alert to Carr's pager, as well as pagers held by two surveillance teams, whenever the e-mail account was accessed, providing the IP address for where it had been accessed from.

The idea was to have surveillance attempt to spot the spy as soon as he logged in to his e-mail account. Carr had drawn up an Excel spreadsheet listing the IP addresses for libraries in the greater Washington, D.C., area—where the spy was likely to return to access the account. Some of the libraries had dynamic IP addresses; to make it simple to track any log-ins from there, the FBI requested that the Internet service providers for those libraries assign them fixed IP addresses. The service providers complied, the library administrators cooperated, and after the arrangements were made, the FBI tested the system around mid-January. Carr's pager flashed as planned. The FBI's surveillance teams took to camping out by the libraries often, anticipating an alert, but as the weeks passed, Carr wondered if the spy was ever going to log in to the account again.

Catching spies isn't always cloak-and-dagger stuff; sometimes it involves endless hours of drudgery. For a couple of weeks that winter, two of Carr's colleagues spent the bulk of their workdays hunched over a desk at the Library of Congress, combing through used-car ads that had appeared in the *Washington Post* over the prior two years. They were looking to find out if any country had already established contact with the spy using the instructions provided. The agents didn't find any ads matching what was described in the letter.

Carr set a plan in motion to draw out the spy, preparing for what's known in counterintelligence as a false-flag operation. The idea was to respond to the letter as the spy had wanted Libyan intelligence to. As Carr and his fellow agents went about following the instructions in the letter, they discovered just how hard the spy had made it to do business with him. If Libyan officials had taken the spy up on his offer, Carr thought, they would likely have slapped their heads in frustration along the way.

The first complication was getting an 800 number as the letter asked for. Carr's squad requested that FBI New York set it up. But every 800 number the agents attempted to acquire was taken. Like good domain names, 800 numbers are a prized commodity, as evidenced by the endless stream of commercials on late-night TV that invite viewers to call toll-free to buy everything from golf clubs to cat food.

"The best we can do is get a 1-888 number," an agent from New York told Carr.

"Let's buy a 1-800 number from somebody," Carr said. "I don't care if it costs $100,000."

The FBI did care, however, and in the end, the investigators settled for an 888 number. But when Carr read the number New York had gotten, he let out a moan of exasperation. It ended in a 0. The spy had asked that the last seven digits of the number be reversed and presented as a local-area phone number in the used-car ad he was going to look out for. It wouldn't make sense for the ad to list a phone number starting with 0.

The FBI had to get a different 888 number. Carr called the *Washington Post*'s classified section to place the ad. He read out the details of the car from the spy's letter: a 1993 Ford Taurus with 95,000 miles on it. Asking price: $17,000.

There was a moment of silence from the other end.

"Sir, no one's going to buy your car for seventeen thousand dollars," the person taking the call said. "That's a crazy asking price."

"Yeah, I know," Carr said. "I still want that in the ad, though."

"Sir, I can't in good conscience advise you to post this ad and expect to sell your car," the person said. "You are wasting your money."

There are times when FBI agents can flash their badges to get something done. This wasn't one of them. "I just want to put a classified ad in your paper," Carr finally said, losing patience. "I've got a credit card here and I'm going to pay. I don't care what your opinion is! So just place the ad, OK?"

He made the payment and hung up.

Next, Carr sent an e-mail to the jacobscall address to inform the spy that he should look out for the ad in a week's time. In the note, sent from an e-mail account created under the pseudonym "Shawn McGuire," Carr wrote, "We got your letter. We are definitely interested in your offer. We set up a 1-888 number instead of a 1-800 number but all else remains the same. Please contact us."

The FBI assigned an Arabic speaker to answer the toll-free number. Then the agents waited, hoping the spy would call.

CHAPTER 2

TRAITOR UNMASKED

O n a snowy day in the middle of January 2001, Gary Walker, an agent with the Air Force Office of Special Investigations, sat hunched over a desk in a windowless room at the National Reconnaissance Office headquarters in Chantilly. The room was the size of a walk-in closet, with barely enough space for a couple of chairs and two small rectangular desks. It was cramped further by a cart that Walker had wheeled into the room. On it was a stack of files containing the personnel records of employees at the NRO.

Walker began reading file after file, jotting down notes on a pad. Weeks earlier, he had entertained the fleeting hope that this weary task wouldn't need to be undertaken. When Steve Carr had briefed the NRO about the spy's letter and accompanying bona fides, Walker's first reaction was to ask if the letter wasn't part of a clever double-agent operation initiated by some entity within the U.S. government—a dangle to win over Libyan intelligence. Like other countries, the United States routinely conducts such operations, in which somebody from the U.S. ranks reaches out to the enemy, masquerading as a spy. Besides creating opportunities for misinforming the enemy and gleaning enemy secrets, double-agent ops are intended to discourage the enemy from accepting volunteer spies.

But Walker's hopes of the letter signifying a dummy threat had been dashed soon enough, after the National Counterintelligence Center checked with the Army, Navy, Air Force, and other organizations and confirmed that it wasn't a double-agent op. Walker, assigned to the NRO from the Air Force Office of Special Investigations, was tasked with conducting personnel reviews to flag potential suspects. The files to be looked at numbered in the thousands, and since they weren't digitized, the only way to review them was by going through them page by page.

Walker steeled himself to the prospect of spending the next several months holed up in that little room. Along with an employee's résumé, history of postings, job description, and performance appraisals, each file contained reports of background investigations done for granting the employee a security clearance. Starting out, Walker scanned the files for traditional counterintelligence indicators. Evidence of financial difficulty, including big debt. Alcoholism or drug addiction. Failure to report foreign travel or contact with foreigners—required of employees holding security clearances. A weighty indicator on the list was problems in clearing a polygraph, or lie detector test, which, although founded on disputed science, remains the government's primary tool for affirming if an employee is answering questions honestly.

In looking for these possible red flags, Walker was following a model built on decades of mole hunts, from which investigators had come up with what they believed were potential signs of an insider's susceptibility to committing espionage, be it willingly or under threat of blackmail.

About a week into the reviews, Walker heard a knock on his door. He looked up to see an elderly man smiling at him.

"Hi, I'm Joe Krofcheck," the man said.

A psychiatrist in his late sixties, Krofcheck had worked at the CIA for decades. He had worked on dozens of mole hunts and counterespionage assessments—exercises carried out after catching a spy to gain insights on what precise factors might have led to the treason. The NRO had asked him to see how Walker was faring with the file reviews.

When Walker told him how he'd been going about it, Krofcheck suggested a more targeted approach. "Think about who would want to do this," Krofcheck said, drawing Walker's attention to the spy's statement in the letter about being close to retirement after twenty years of service. That suggested the person was an enlisted service member, Krofcheck said, not an officer or a civilian employee, since only enlisted members face retirement at the end of twenty years. Based on that reasoning, Krofcheck suggested limiting the file reviews to enlisted personnel of grade E-6 or above who had retired within the last two years or were due to retire in the next two years.

Walker's task suddenly became a lot more manageable. He'd been looking at the whole universe of NRO employees, former and current, numbering in the tens of thousands; now he had to scrutinize only a few hundred files. Studying them one cartload at a time, Walker set aside files that met some of the counterintelligence indicators on his list, from financial issues to murky polygraphs.

His attention was first drawn to an employee who had failed to disclose an extramarital affair with a coworker when stationed in Italy. In the same batch of files, Walker came across another person he found interesting: a signals analyst who had retired a few months earlier, in August 2000, at the rank of master sergeant. The person had reported having financial difficulties in the past, but what made Walker pay closer attention to him was something else. Unlike most employees in the pool Walker was looking at, the master sergeant had received training in cryptology. Walker placed the file on top of his stack of candidate suspects. The rest of the files he loaded back onto the cart and wheeled out of the room, only to return minutes later with the next cartload.

Like Walker at the NRO, counterintelligence officials at the NSA and the CIA were combing through their agencies' ranks to find persons of interest. The FBI had named the investigation Cast About, in a reference to the spy's gambit to market himself to the Libyans. It was clear that a classic counterintelligence review of employee records at the three agencies was going to be a slow, painstaking effort that would take months.

Carr had to think of other investigative avenues to pursue in the meantime. Possibly the strongest clue available to him and his fellow agents was the set of nineteen documents the spy had down-loaded from Intelink. Shortly after the hunt began, one of Carr's colleagues on the squad—an agent named Bill Lace—set about tracing each of the documents to the Intelink sites they had been printed from.

A mild-mannered man of slight build, Lace was a civil engineer by training who had followed in the footsteps of his wife, Andrea Price-Lace, to join the bureau in the late nineties. He had never had any reason to use Intelink before. An analyst in the Washington Field Office helped him get a log-in, and in short order, Lace found himself sitting in front of a computer in a tightly controlled space for the handling and processing of classified information—what's known as a Sensitive Compartmented Information Facility or SCIF—and surfing an Internet hidden from public view.

Intelink sprang into existence in 1994, as corporations and academic institutions around the world were beginning to harness the power of the World Wide Web. James Woolsey, then director of Central Intelligence—a title that at the time made him head of both the CIA and the broader intelligence community—wanted the government's large and diverse ensemble of intel agencies to work better with one other. It was common to hear of different entities not wanting to share information, and the DCI's solution was to link up the digitized databases of these agencies and form a shared network of servers that would allow for exchanging, utilizing, and building on intelligence developed by different players.

Searching on Intelink, Lace soon found the URLs for each of the nineteen documents. The next step was to find out who had accessed all of these sites over the previous two years. It might have been an easy task if all the documents had resided on one central server. But as Lace learned, that wasn't the case.

Each of the documents was stored on the server of the specific agency where it had been created. Every agency maintained its own log of network traffic stemming from within and outside the agency, and the traffic originating from one entity sometimes went through a number of intermediate servers before arriving at the destination server, where the requested document resided. To complicate matters further, the way logs of network traffic were kept wasn't uniform across agencies. Tracing accesses to the nineteen documents would require a massive audit of these logs.

Lace reached out to the IT administrators of the NSA, CIA,

NRO, and other organizations, requesting that they scrutinize the traffic to and from their servers for six of the nineteen documents. Despite focusing on this subset of URLs, it took more than two weeks for the agencies to start getting back to the FBI with results. What Lace heard from them was disheartening. In the two years prior, the six documents had been accessed by hundreds of people across the intel community. Many had accessed several—if not all—of the documents. There was no way to single out any one person.

Doing the same thing over and over and expecting a different result is how some define insanity. By that definition, Carr was unquestionably going insane as he developed the investigation through the first few weeks of 2001. Although he'd already spent hours studying the materials the spy had mailed to the embassy, Carr returned to his binder almost compulsively to look at the letter and the bona fides package again and again.

One morning, as he sat at his desk flipping through those pages, Carr noticed what looked like a smear of telex ink running across the top edge of one of the documents. It was a CIA report titled "Gaddhafi's Undependable Pragmatism."

When Carr looked closely, he could see that the line was in fact a string of text. It wasn't legible, though, because the upper half of the text was cut off. Only the bottom half of the string appeared on the page. Still, Carr could make out that the fragment was from the document's header, which for a Web page typically indicates the site's URL along with other information. None of the other documents had anything like it at their top or their bottom, suggesting that the spy had taken care to scrub any headers and footers, either before or after printing them out. Somehow, he seemed to have failed to do so for this CIA report.

When Carr took a moment to look up from his desk, he caught sight of a colleague from another FBI office who happened to be visiting the Washington Field Office that morning. The colleague, a special agent whose first name was Jack, belonged to an FBI unit that specializes in secretly entering buildings and cars—with court authorization—to assist investigations that need to be conducted covertly. In the bureau, these covert entry experts are called the "flaps-and-seals" guys.

In Carr's view of the world, Jack's presence near his cubicle at precisely the moment when Carr had been squinting at the illegible string on the CIA document wasn't a mere coincidence. As Carr would come to see it in the months ahead, it was yet another example of divine providence.

"Hey, Jack, come here, check this out," Carr called out. He'd worked with Jack in the past and knew that Jack's expertise went beyond making covert entries.

He showed Jack the document, drawing his attention to the line at the top. "I thought maybe it was a copier error or something, but I think this is a string of text," Carr said. "Do you think you could recover it?"

"Absolutely," Jack said. "Give me a copy of it and I'll run down to the lab."

He left shortly after and, about three hours later, e-mailed Carr with the results. Using a combination of guesswork and digital technology, he had built out the sliced-off portion of the text, completing each partial character. Carr now had a legible header.

The URL of the report wasn't what he was after; he already

knew that. What the header also included was the date the document had been printed on: July 8, 1999.

Carr knew at once the utility of this information. It meant that investigators could now attempt a focused search for computers that had accessed the CIA report on a specific day, rather than over a two-year period, assuming that the spy had looked up the document on the same day that he had printed it.

And so, while IT administrators at various intel agencies were discovering hundreds of accesses to the six documents that the FBI had asked them to check for in their network traffic, Carr requested that the National Security Agency lead an Intelink audit aimed at identifying computers that had accessed the CIA report on July 8, 1999. Right before March, Carr got the audit results back from the NSA. The document had been accessed on that particular day by eleven IP addresses. Six of them stemmed from contractors on the West Coast, which Carr ruled out since the spy had to be somewhere in the D.C. area. Of the remaining accesses, two had stemmed from the NSA and one from inside the CIA. The other two computers to have accessed the document belonged to the National Reconnaissance Office.

At the NRO, Gary Walker dug deeper into the backgrounds of the nearly thirty employees he had identified through his file reviews as persons of interest. The closer he looked, the more interested he became in the Air Force master sergeant who had retired in August 2000.

The serviceman's training and postings as a signals analyst told Walker that he likely had in-depth knowledge of satellite reconnaissance. There was something else that caught Walker's eye. It was a rebuttal the analyst had written in 1988 in response to a less-than-stellar performance appraisal. What struck Walker was that it was filled with misspellings.

Written on a typewriter, the three-page letter was titled "Rebutal." The missing *t* was no anomaly, nor had it been skipped over in a fit of frenzied typing. As Walker read on, he encountered wrong spellings in almost every line; even the word "the" was scrambled into "teh" in some places. He was also surprised by the strident tone of the letter. It seemed disproportionately severe compared to the mild criticisms in the appraisal. The writer had gone on at great length about how exceptional his work was and how his supervisor—a woman—did not deserve to be a manager.

Walker shared the rebuttal with Krofcheck, the psychiatrist. The two compared it with the letter the spy had written to the embassy. It wasn't just that both texts were riddled with misspellings. Krofcheck saw similarities between the two in the way that certain words had been misspelled. The analyst and the spy both seemed to have a tendency to transpose letters, for example, spelling "proceed" as "procede"—an error frequently made by those with dyslexia.

Krofcheck pointed out a deeper similarity between the rebuttal and the letter to the embassy. In both, Krofcheck heard the angry voice of grievance, of somebody who felt the world hadn't given him his due.

In early March, Walker learned the results of the Intelink audit, showing that the CIA report printed on July 8, 1999, had been accessed by five IP addresses from the CIA, NSA, and NRO. Investigators had not been able to trace the two accesses from the NRO all the way to the specific computers that had downloaded the document, but to nodal points in the NRO's internal network, each of which fed into a work suite consisting of a handful of computers. Walker compiled a list of NRO employees who had worked at these two suites: one at the headquarters in Chantilly, the other at an NRO office located thirty miles away, near I-295 in Maryland.

The Air Force master sergeant had worked at both locations. Walker picked up the phone and called the FBI's Washington Field Office.

Bill Lace took the call.

"Hi, Bill," Walker said. "This is Gary."

The two men had discussed the investigation a few times during the prior weeks. But from the tone of Walker's voice, Lace could tell that this was more than a routine update.

Walker told him about the master sergeant. He listed all the reasons that made the man a strong suspect in his eyes: the position of signals analyst, the cryptology training, the misspellings in the rebuttal letter, the date of his retirement relative to when the envelopes had been mailed to the embassy. And finally, most compellingly, the fact that the master sergeant had worked at the two NRO work suites from which the top secret CIA assessment of Muammar Gaddhafi had been accessed in July 1999.

"I think this is our guy," Walker told Lace.

Lace asked where the master sergeant lived. Walker read out the retiree's home address. It was in Bowie, in Prince George's County, Maryland, in close proximity to the libraries that the jacobscall e-mail address had been accessed from. To Lace, that was further confirmation that Walker had identified a strong candidate.

In the weeks leading up to March, the squad had opened preliminary investigations into a handful of other suspects who had been identified through file reviews at the NSA and the CIA. The FBI had given these individuals code names that reflected the overarching case: one suspect, who worked at the CIA, was referred to as Cast-A-Line; another, from the NSA, was labeled Cast Short; a third, also from the NSA, was given the name Cast Arrow.

Some of these preliminary investigations had already reached their logical end, eliminating certain suspects from the running. For instance, when investigators matched up Cast-A-Line's absences from the CIA with the times when the jacobscall e-mail account had been checked, they were convinced he wasn't their man. In one instance, the analysis showed, the person would have had to drive out of the CIA in Langley, Virginia, over to a library in Oxon Hill, Maryland, log in and out of the e-mail account, and return to the CIA all in a matter of twenty minutes. "He probably stepped out to get a sandwich," Carr had concluded.

After the phone call from Walker, Lace poked his head into Carr's cubicle and told him what he had learned. The FBI launched a preliminary investigation on the master sergeant on March 15, 2001, assigning him the code name Cast Led.

Like Lace and Walker, Carr thought the serviceman looked promising, but he wasn't willing to bet on Cast Led just yet. He had seen from close range the folly of locking onto a target prematurely in a counterespionage investigation. Just a few months earlier, the FBI had discovered that its agents had made a grave error in pursuing the CIA's Brian Kelly for years on the suspicion that he had been passing secrets to the Russians when the mole they should have gone after was the FBI's own Robert Hanssen. To be certain about Cast Led, Carr needed more evidence.

Late in the evening on March 28, Carr parked his car in front of a Dunkin' Donuts in Chantilly, Virginia, and walked inside. If

Carr had been a cop on neighborhood patrol, stepping into a doughnut shop for a cup of coffee would have been a cliché. As it was, though, Carr was at the store to meet up with other federal agents in preparation for a key mission. Their task for the night was to conduct a secret search of an office at the NRO headquarters. To catch a spy, Carr liked to say, it was sometimes necessary to hide in the weeds and move only at night.

The men leading the operation were the FBI's covert entry specialists. Among them was Carr's friend Jack, who had helped the hunt previously by reconstituting the header of the CIA report in the spy's bona fides. Jack and his flaps-and-seals colleagues had broken into dozens of homes and cars and buildings over the years to assist with investigations of every manner at the FBI. To carry out these break-ins, always authorized by a court order, the specialists often had to prepare for weeks, watching the comings and goings of residents in the immediate vicinity of a targeted house, for instance, to find the right time to enter without alerting neighbors. They were used to walking around furniture in dark rooms in the dead of night, sometimes aided by nothing more than a flashlight covered with a red filter to soften the beam so that people driving by wouldn't notice any activity through the windows. The aim was to execute a ghostlike entry and exit, leaving no trace behind that might alert the target of the investigation.

Tonight's mission was a bit different from most break-ins. It was unusual for Jack and his colleagues to facilitate a clandestine entry at another government agency. The plan wasn't entirely secret to the NRO; the FBI had briefed counterintelligence officials at the NRO about the plan, which was to examine all the computers in the suite at NRO headquarters that the Intelink audit had pointed to. Gary Walker was accompanying the search team, and NRO managers had already given the FBI the keys to enter the main building where the suite was located. Yet the operation had to be done covertly, because if any of the NRO employees working in the suite were to find out, the spy could be alerted.

Carr had done his own share of planning for the night. He knew that the suite had four computers—the machine from which the CIA report had been accessed could have been any one of them. But copying the hard drives of four computers—to allow each to be combed through later—wasn't going to be easy all in one night with the limited amount of equipment Carr's squad had available to deploy. And so, Carr had asked computer forensics experts from the NSA to help.

Shortly after eleven p.m., the FBI agents and other members of the team exited Dunkin' Donuts and drove to the NRO, a cavalcade of cars speeding through the night. After they had driven around the NRO building and verified that nobody was inside, the men parked in a lower-level garage. They took an elevator down to the basement and walked down a hallway to get to the suite.

Carr stepped in and surveyed the space. It had four large cubicles, each with its own desktop. Jack and his colleagues began taking Polaroid pictures, recording the position of every object in the room, from how paperweights and staplers lay on the desks to how the wheels at the bottoms of the chairs were turned. The computer forensics team set up two plastic folding tables in an adjacent room. Agents carefully unplugged the four computers and lugged them over to the makeshift workstation, where the forensics experts hooked each of them up to disk-imaging hardware to copy the contents of each hard drive.

As the imaging got under way, Carr sprawled out on the floor and caught up on some sleep, with the computers whirring in the background. In the early hours of the morning, the flaps-and-seals agents nudged him awake. The men put the computers back where they belonged, folded up the tables, and got ready to leave. Using the Polaroid shots as a reference, they ensured that the suite looked exactly as it had when they had walked in. Carr gathered up the photographs, all of which had been numbered, to make sure they weren't leaving any of them behind.

He couldn't account for all the pictures. One, number 26, appeared to be missing.

"Oh, crap," he said.

Jack looked at him sternly.

Carr went over the pictures again. The men looked around on the desks and the floor but couldn't find any photographs lying around.

"I think I misnumbered the pictures," Carr said finally. He had skipped 26 when writing down numbers on the backs of the pictures in serial order.

Jack was furious. "How could you have done that?" he asked. For a flaps-and-seals operation, a slip like that was a cardinal sin.

Carr apologized. He had been working eighteen-hour days since the spy hunt began. The grind of the investigation was fraying his nerves.

Jack didn't talk to him for the remainder of the operation. It was dawn when the men drove out of the building with the hard drive images. Carr went home and sank into bed, exhausted.

It was past noon when Carr woke up and left for work. While he was on his way, he got a phone call from the computer forensics team at the NSA. While Carr slept, they had examined the four hard drives imaged from the NRO.

"We found some stuff," the caller said.

"I'll call you back from a secure phone," Carr said. He hung up and drove as fast as he could to get to the Washington Field Office. He bounded up the stairs and dialed the NSA on a special landline that government agencies use for calls that need to be especially protected from eavesdropping.

On one of the four hard drives, the forensics team had found URLs of what they believed to be some of the Intelink documents in the bona fides package. Lace went to the NSA that afternoon to look at the URLs himself, since he was the one who had located each of those sites on Intelink previously. He called Carr shortly after to give him the report.

Twelve of the hundreds of URLs cached on the hard drive matched the nineteen that Lace had on his list. Among them was the CIA report printed on July 8, 1999. The last person who had used the computer was Cast Led. Nobody had logged in to it since Cast Led had retired in August 2000.

"Are you kidding me?" Carr asked excitedly. "Oh my God, we actually have a primary suspect."

On the night of April 2, Carr went back to the NRO for a second entry into the suite, this time accompanied by experts from the FBI's Computer Analysis and Response Team. Unlike the previous night, the CART personnel focused on the desktop that Cast Led had worked on until a few months before. While they imaged the hard drive, following special protocols for preserving digital evidence, Carr and other agents looked around the suite.

On an overhead shelf in the cubicle where Cast Led had worked, an agent found the manual *Joint Tactical Exploitation of National Systems*, a handbook containing descriptions of U.S. spy satellites and other intelligence-gathering equipment. The spy had included the manual's table of contents in the bona fides package and had offered to sell information contained in it. The agent picked up the manual and showed it to Carr.

Carr opened it. Inside, on the cover page, written in block letters with a marker pen, was the name of the retired master sergeant.

Brian Patrick Regan.

The worst nightmare for officials in charge of security and counterintelligence at an intelligence agency is to find out that the safeguards they have had in place to protect against insider threats were simply not good enough. For weeks, NRO's managers had hoped against hope that the spy would turn out to be from the ranks of a different organization. But with the discovery of the URLs of the bona fide documents on the computer in the NRO suite, the agency's fears had been realized.

The aerial pictures of Gaddhafi's yacht had provided additional confirmation that the sender of the package was none other than Regan. Analysts had determined that the photographs, taken by a foreign intelligence agency, were among materials that were given out at an intelligence course that Regan had attended at Colorado Springs in the summer of 1997. Only one other individual from the NRO had attended the course.

From everything that investigators had learned about Regan, he seemed like an unlikely spy. Six feet four inches tall, he towered over most colleagues, although only by virtue of his height, not on account of personality or apparent intellect. If anything, his lumbering, giantlike frame and his halting style of conversation gave him the appearance of a man who could never be swift in action or in thought. The impression was solidified by Regan's social awkwardness, which his coworkers took to be the reason behind his reclusive nature.

Yet, despite the doltish persona and the muddled spelling, Regan had evidently masterminded a sophisticated espionage plot, one that might have been impossible to discover if it hadn't been for the lucky break the FBI got from its informant. It was all the more stunning that Regan had been able to give effect to his conspiracy without raising any suspicions at what was perhaps the most se-cretive and security-conscious of U.S. intelligence agencies.

But what was the extent of the man's plot? What had Regan gotten away with so far, and what was he planning to do next?

The first step toward answering those questions was to assemble a full picture of Regan's activities on Intelink. During much of the twentieth century, spies looking for information to pass on to their masters had to steal dossiers from cabinet lockers, pilfer blueprints stored on microfiche, and snap hurried photographs of military plans left on a general's desk. But times had changed. All that Regan would have needed to do to find sellable secrets, investigators real-ized, was sit in his cubicle and surf the intelligence community's classified intranet.

NRO's counterintelligence chief, Debra Donahoo, asked the agen-cy's IT administrators to examine what Regan had accessed on Intelink in the two years before he retired. The job required forensics expertise that the NRO didn't have in-house. Donahoo called the Air Force Office of Special Investigations for help, and AFOSI sent over a young digital forensics investigator named Bret Padres.

Padres was a soft-spoken man with a square face topped by a

thick mat of jet-black hair. On a rainy spring morning, he arrived at the NRO headquarters and walked through the security turnstiles to meet up with a network administrator named Bill Green in the agency's IT department. Green led him to a room crowded with binders containing reams and reams of computer printouts. The printouts, Green explained, were the records of network traffic at the NRO. Green had been going through them manually in an attempt to identify the traffic to Regan's computer.

The logs were derived from a device the size of a pizza box, called an Automated Security Incident Measurement (ASIM) system. Developed in the 1990s to improve computer security on Air Force bases and in other Air Force–related institutions, ASIM devices sat at the firewalls of the computer networks within the NRO, recording the traffic going in and out of each network. Padres was familiar with the system. In a previous posting at the Air Force Academy, he had been used to getting phone calls from the Air Force Computer Emergency Response team—a group based in San Antonio, Texas—asking him to analyze ASIM data to look for indicators of a network attack.

At the NRO, the logs of network traffic were backed up from the ASIMs onto digital tapes every night. The NRO had some four years' worth of tapes in its archives. Up until this point, they had simply taken up valuable office space. But now the decision to store them suddenly seemed prescient.

Going through their contents on paper would have taken the better part of a year, Padres told Donahoo. He suggested taking the data with him to a lab where he and others would be able to analyze it more quickly.

The NRO wasn't used to letting anybody take information out of the building—officially, anyway. It took Donahoo nearly two weeks to get all the approvals. Padres had the tapes transported to the Defense Computer Forensics Lab in Linthicum, Maryland, where he was given a secure space, equipped to handle classified information, to do the analysis.

Working with two colleagues from AFOSI, Padres first loaded the tapes onto hard drives. Donahoo had pressed for urgency, and the men worked in shifts around the clock, taking naps in a hotel room across the street. After the data had been transferred, Padres wrote a number of programs to search through it in different ways.

The analysis showed that Regan had been an avid surfer of Intelink, spending hours on it every day. His surfing pattern was in sharp contrast to those of coworkers in the suite and elsewhere at the NRO. The others accessed Intelink less frequently and for shorter durations, browsing only a handful of topics relating to their assignments. Regan had explored the entire landscape, looking at a diverse set of reports, imagery, and analysis pertaining to multiple countries. His searches were literally all over the map—"Top Secret Iran," "Top Secret Iraq." In some instances, he'd misspelled the keywords he was searching for—for example, spelling "Libya" as "Lybia" or "Libia."

It was apparent right away that the nineteen documents in the bona fides package, which he had accessed numerous times, were simply the tip of the iceberg. Regan had looked at hundreds, possibly thousands, of documents. Using special software, Padres plotted the Intelink activity on a graph, overlaying it with Regan's badging records, which indicated when he'd entered and exited the NRO. The surfing coincided with his work attendance, confirming that nobody else had been logging on to Regan's desktop to browse Intelink.

Sometime in mid-April, Donahoo and other counterintelligence officials from the NRO visited Linthicum for a presentation that Padres had put together. Carr was in attendance as well, along with other agents from the Washington Field Office. Padres hooked up his laptop to a projector and clicked through the graphs he had plotted. In one of them, each document that Regan had accessed on Intelink was represented as a dot, and documents related to a single topic were clustered together. The picture evoked a patch of sky imaged by a telescope, each swarm of dots resembling a galaxy. This is what espionage in the digital age looked like.

Using software called NetworkMiner, Padres had extracted from the network traffic the hundreds upon hundreds of satellite images and intelligence reports that Regan had browsed. For the presentation, he had created a slide show that flashed each of the images and the cover pages of the remaining documents in rapid succession. Watching the slides roll one after another on the screen, Donahoo and her colleagues from the NRO were stunned. Though each slide appeared for a second or less, the entire show could have run for hours. The sheer volume of material blew everybody's mind.

"How was he able to access this stuff?" Donahoo kept asking, shaking her head in disbelief. It was more an expression of shock than a genuine question.

"There are no restrictions on Intelink," Padres replied, stating the obvious. "He was able to download anything he wanted."

Regan's nefarious surfing had gone on, completely unnoticed, for more than a year before his retirement. He'd proved to be the perfect insider threat, underestimated and ignored, left to operate stealthily in the shadows. The more Carr learned about him, the more intriguing he found the mismatch between Regan's unrefined exterior and his hidden cunning. Who was this unusual adversary and what secrets had he stolen?

CHAPTER 3

THE ROOTS OF DYSFUNCTION

Long before Brian Regan decided to commit espionage against the United States, long before he entered the Air Force, and long before his atrocious spelling invited mocking from friends in school, life taught him that he had to fend for himself to survive. It's a lesson that everybody must learn, and Regan was forced to learn it early, as a young blond-haired boy growing up in Farmingdale, a small town in the center of Long Island, New York.

Regan's parents, Michael and Anne, were Irish immigrants who had moved to the United States in the fifties in search of a better life. They struggled to raise their brood of eight children on Michael's modest income as a worker at a factory that made twist drills. Regan, the third child of the family and the oldest of five brothers, knew from a young age that he'd have to compete with his siblings for food, space, and parental attention in a household where all three were in short supply. He grew out his toenails so that he could use them as little daggers to make more room for himself in the bed he shared for a while with one of his brothers. As an adolescent, he put padlocks on his closet to guard his cookies and Pop-Tarts from his siblings. It was as if he were living in a jungle where nobody else was going to look out for him. Survival depended on outsmarting the world. Regan was on his own.

The Regans lived in a small house on Lois Lane in the southern part of Farmingdale, in a neighborhood of blue-collar workers untouched by privilege. Michael had added a second floor to the house, doing much of the construction himself, to accommodate his and Anne's burgeoning brood of children. Still, for a family with ten members—not counting two dogs—the living space afforded by the home was decidedly cramped. There wasn't enough room around the dinner table for everybody to sit down together, and so it wasn't unusual for the kids to eat in shifts, except on holidays, when extra chairs were brought in to make everyone fit. During late spring and summer, when the mornings were warm, Regan would sometimes turn on the hose in the backyard and take a shower there. With so many siblings needing to use the two bathrooms in the house at that hour, on certain days it was the only way to get ready for school on time.

Regan's father was a powerfully built man with a thick Irish accent that refused to fade even after decades in the United States. He drank more than was good for him, and not just on Saint Patrick's Day, when he would go out to the pub with friends to celebrate his Irish roots. He loved playing records of old Irish melodies at home. By most accounts, he wasn't much of a conversationalist. His preference was to drown his frustrations in alcohol rather than to talk about them. Like many fathers of his generation, he was an intimidating presence at home and didn't hesitate to hand out corporal punishment when he lost his patience with the children.

While commotion often reigned in the house in his absence, the atmosphere was a lot more subdued when he was around.

Michael and Anne had both had a strict Catholic upbringing, and they strived to make religion an important part of their family's life. On Sunday mornings, the Regans would get dressed and cram into the family's station wagon to drive to church, where Anne, wearing a veil over her head, guided her girls and boys into the pews.

The job of raising the kids fell mostly on her. She sent Regan to a Catholic school in the neighboring town of Massapequa, hoping that the strict environment there would help build his character. Regan didn't respond well to the school's stern discipline and often got into trouble. Once, he was admonished for bringing a pack of playing cards to school—a forbidden item. In fourth grade, he began smuggling candy into class to sell to his peers. Candy, too, wasn't allowed in class, which made it an especially valued commodity, like cigarettes in prison. Regan was able to sell his contraband taffies, called Now & Laters—for a tidy profit.

Regan didn't last at the school beyond fourth grade, however. One day, he and three of his friends were playing tag at the altar of the school chapel. As they ran around, one of the boys swung himself around a giant candlestick that stood in the middle of the altar, forgetting that it wasn't some kind of lamppost attached to the floor. The candlestick toppled and was smashed to pieces. In the eyes of the Lord, the damage caused may have been a forgivable sin; in the view of the nuns who ran the school, it wasn't. Regan, along with two of the other kids, was expelled.

For a boy who was not yet ten years old, being kicked out of school was a shameful and traumatic experience. Even before adolescence, when most people find the innocence of childhood slipping away, Regan was learning that the world could be an unkind place. The expulsion was proof that society was an adversary from which no sympathy could be expected.

As Regan grew into his teens, that outlook was hardened by an abusive father at home. The fear of getting a beating from Michael, for the smallest of infractions, was never far from his mind. One afternoon, Regan was playing with a friend in the woods, when he slipped and fell into a stream. It had been raining and the water was high. He was completely soaked. Regan's friend helped him get out. (I shall refer to this friend, who asked not to be identified by his real name, as Tom.)

"I'll get my ass kicked if I go home like this," Regan said, sounding panicked.

"Come over to my house," Tom said.

Regan was relieved. Tom's mother had him change and got his clothes washed and dried. It was getting late, so she called Regan's house to ask if he could stay for dinner. When the permission was granted, she served him a meal of chicken, rice, and green beans.

"What is that?" Regan asked, pointing at the rice. He'd never encountered rice before: the menu at home rarely strayed from a traditional Irish meat-and-potatoes theme. After dinner was done, he changed back into his clothes and walked home, thankful to not have to face his father's wrath.

By the time Regan entered middle school, it was evident to his teachers that he was a slow learner. To call him a C student might have been generous. The reason for Regan's consistently poor academic performance was dyslexia, a learning disorder that makes it difficult for the brain to process and remember a sequence of written characters, be they letters or numbers. Millions of people around the world suffer from the disorder; one out of every twenty people in the United States is dyslexic. Like others with the disability, Regan struggled to read and write, and as is typical for many dyslexics, he also had difficulties learning math, which—just like reading—requires the interpretation of strings of alphabetical and numerical text.

Dyslexia is a problem of visual and auditory processing; it does not imply low intelligence. Nonetheless, dyslexic children are often perceived by their peers and teachers as being intellectually inferior. In a culture where reading and writing are the primary gateway to academic success, it's not hard to see why. During reading sessions in class, when the teacher goes around the room calling on individual students to read passages aloud, the dyslexic kid feels a rising sense of dread. While most other students get through the exercise with little effort, he stumbles through his lines, wincing at the chuckles and uncomfortable silences that punctuate his slow, painful reading.

Attending Mill Lane Junior High, Regan experienced these trials on a routine basis. He was assigned to remedial classes along with other students with various learning and behavioral challenges. Back then, teachers and school administrators were less attuned to dyslexia and other disabilities, and by most accounts, students like Regan did not receive sufficient targeted help to overcome the specific problems they faced. "We were just seen as troubled students that didn't want to learn or pay attention," recalls Peter Klopfer, a classmate of Regan's who, like him, had a reading disability. Regan, like Klopfer, rarely talked to others in class and made every effort to be invisible. As Klopfer explains, "You wouldn't really want to speak out even if you thought you knew the answer. If the teacher called on you, you'd dummy up or say—I don't know. You wouldn't want to be put on the spot."

Dyslexia doesn't affect just academic performance. It can destroy a child's social standing. Over time, it can induce a permanent sense of being an outsider, of being on the margins. Some dyslexics are able to overcome this constant bruising to their self-esteem by excelling outside the classroom, in sports, for instance. Some are able to cope because they have exceptional support from their parents.

Regan didn't find any such refuge. He wasn't much of an athlete and didn't play any sport well enough to earn the respect of his peers. The kids he hung out with in his neighborhood would often gang up on him. His affectations, his speech, and the jokes he made always seemed out of step with the others, making him an easy target for mocking. He would come up with one-liners and then break into a cackling, hyena-like laugh that the other kids usually found funnier than the joke. "He was a little bit odd," recalls Cliff Wagner, who was part of the clique. "We used to laugh at him more than with him."

Like many teenage boys of the day, Regan took up delivering newspapers to earn pocket money. On weekdays, after school ended in the afternoon, he would ride his bicycle over to the County Line Shopping Center with a friend and wait for the newspaper truck to arrive. After stacks of the *Long Island Press*, an evening paper, had been hauled off the truck and onto the sidewalk, Regan—like the other carriers—would load up his bicycle with two large bundles of newspapers—one in the front basket, one in the back—and set out on his delivery route. It wasn't an easy ride, especially on Thursdays, when the paper was nearly twice the regular size because of an additional section, and on Sunday mornings, when it was fattened further by pullouts and supplements. He'd park his bicycle at every house he had to deliver to, walk up to the front step, and leave the paper on the porch or in the mailbox. The work paid about $40 per week.

It was good money, but Regan had to work for every cent of

it—more so than the others because of all the bullying he had to put up with on the route. The neighborhood kids, Wagner leading the pack, would throw roof shingles at him. They would knock his bike down, spilling the newspapers on the ground, and run, laughing. Regan would chase after them, yelling his pet curse: "Son of a bitch." Everybody knew it was a hopeless pursuit—not only was Regan slow on his feet; he wasn't very well coordinated in his movements. In the winter months, the chase would end with him slipping and falling on the ice while the bullies enjoyed the spectacle from a distance.

Regan felt increasingly frustrated and powerless, and one day, he decided he couldn't take it anymore. After what had been an especially humiliating afternoon, he got hold of a BB gun and went after one of his tormentors, a boy named Bob Florio, who was watching TV at a friend's house. Hearing the commotion, the father of the friend, a beefy man named Joe, came out. Regan was in the driveway, brandishing the gun.

"What are you going to do with that gun, boy?" Joe asked.

"That guy, that son of a bitch, he terrorizes me on my paper route," Regan yelled in fury, referring to Bob Florio. "He tries to make me run every time, and I fall."

"Go home, boy," Joe advised.

Regan finally left, unable to exact his revenge. Instead of giving him a tough-guy reputation, the story of the incident—told and retold by kids on the block—served to reinforce Regan's image as an oddball and a clown, somebody not worth taking seriously.

According to the theory of multiple intelligences, put forth by the Harvard psychologist Howard Gardner in 1983, the human race is endowed with nine kinds of intelligence. Our education system has traditionally rewarded only two of them: verbal or linguistic intelligence and the intelligence for mathematical thinking and logical reasoning. Gardner goes beyond these to list seven others. There are musical intelligence and bodily-kinesthetic intelligence, which dancers and athletes possess in spades. There are intrapersonal or social intelligence, which successful politicians ride on, and interpersonal intelligence, the ability for self-awareness that is the hallmark of spiritual figures. There's naturalistic intelligence—the aptitude for observing and understanding nature. And then there's spatial intelligence—the talent for visual thinking, memory, and imagination that architects, artists, and sculptors rely on.

Regan would have scored poorly in many of these categories: he was obviously not verbally gifted or musically inclined, nor was he a graceful athlete or socially outgoing. But if there was one talent that he seemed to possess in abundance, it was spatial intelligence. Starting in junior high, he made dozens of intricate ceramic figurines, spending hours carving their features to perfection. Some of the statues were of little bears; others were of Disney characters like Mickey Mouse and Tinker Bell. To guard them from being smashed by the brother closest to him in age, he would store the figurines carefully in the same padlocked closet in which he stashed all kinds of confections to satisfy his sweet tooth. In junior high, he excelled in carpentry class, once helping a classmate make an eagle. Though he wasn't a fan of the written word, he loved comics. He built up a large collection of two of the day's popular comic magazines—*Crazy* and *Cracked*—whose off-the-wall characters delighted him no end and became a source of some of his one-liners.

While delivering newspapers, Regan became friends with Michael Gould, a smiling, cherubic teenager who lived a few blocks away. A year younger than Regan, Gould didn't have any of the meanness that Regan was used to encountering, and the two started spending a lot of time together. On the weekends, they would bike over to the movie-plex at Sunrise Mall, lock up their bikes, and binge-watch as many movies as they could, one after another. "We'd pay for a matinee show, and when it was over, go into another theater, and then another till the night," Gould recalled. "Then we would ride home." For Regan, being away from his house, where he had little privacy, was itself rewarding; watching stars lead fantasy lives on the screen in what constituted hours and hours of entertainment for a couple of bucks was a bonus. He especially enjoyed James Bond movies. Every time they watched one—*The Spy Who Loved Me* was a favorite—he'd remark to Gould how cool the cars and the women in the film were.

The movies were only a temporary escape from the humiliations Regan faced in real life. At school, he continued to struggle to get a passing grade. "I can't believe you graduated," a classmate wrote in his junior high school yearbook in 1977, the year he exited Mill Lane and entered Farmingdale High School. Anyone who borrowed a book from him in class couldn't help chuckling at the misspellings in the notes he had made in the margins. "What the hell are you writing here, Brian?" a friend recalled saying to him. "You've spelled everything wrong!" In the social circle of teenagers in the neighborhood, the likes of Cliff Wagner called him a "retard."

Yet even they felt that Regan possessed an odd ingenuity. He always seemed to have a plan, even though it was usually a bad one, like the time when he traded the perfectly good throttle on his minibike for a lawn mower shifter. The throttle—mounted on the handlebar—allowed for speeding up and slowing down, but Regan wanted to get to full throttle in one step, which he was able to do with the shifter. But he now had less control than before, and moreover, since the shifter was next to the gas tank, close to the ground, he had to bend down while riding at full speed to turn the engine off. Nobody at the mud tracks where the boys raced their minibikes thought Regan had made a good trade.

There were times when his ideas worked out. He once got a pair of rabbits and kept them in a cage in his backyard. Nobody had advised him to keep the male and female rabbit away from each other, and soon enough, the rabbits multiplied. Within weeks, he had more than twenty of them. Regan found a way to use the bounty to mow the lawn. He put them out on the grass, confining four or five of them each under a milk crate. When the animals were done nibbling all the grass under their feet, he slid the crates to another spot, denuding the lawn section by section.

What few of Regan's friends were aware of was his knack for stealth and his willingness to deploy it. One winter evening, when he was still in junior high, Regan broke into a house in the neighborhood. The owners, who were moving to another state, had been gone for a few months. The neighboring house belonged to the family of Regan's friend Tom, whose mother had made him dinner the day he got wet in the stream. She was walking her dog when she noticed, in the darkness, the silhouette of somebody climbing out of the neighbor's window and running away. She rushed into her own house, and Tom's father ran out with a baseball bat to see who it was, but there was nobody to be found. The window of the neighbor's house had been broken.

The police came and discovered that the house had been robbed. All that had been taken were ceramic paints and brushes and carving tools, worth less than a couple of hundred dollars. The police didn't ever track down the thief. But years later, Regan would confess to Tom that the shadowy figure his mother had seen on that cold, dark evening was none other than him.

Sometime around his fifteenth birthday, Regan hit a growth spurt, shooting up to over six feet in height. He'd always been of average size and build compared to kids his age; now he was one of the biggest boys in his cohort, towering over most of his classmates at Farmingdale High. He began working out at the gym. As he grew in physique, so did his confidence. After years of being ridiculed, he was realizing that he had the strength to fight back, and he wasn't afraid to flaunt it.

One winter afternoon, a friend of Regan's named Brian Wagner— who called Regan "Big Irish Mick"—went with him to watch a movie. On the way back, the two decided it would be fun to throw snowballs at a store near the movie theater. The owner of the store, who happened to see them in the act, was not amused. He came out and, along with his son, knocked Brian Wagner off his feet and pinned him to the ground.

Regan pounced on the two attackers and pulled them off Wagner. He threw the store owner down and wrapped his arm around the man's neck, putting him in a tight choke hold. All those years of wrestling with his brother on the front lawn of his house, combined with his newfound strength, were enough to make the fight a no contest.

"Grow up, man, grow up," Regan said, breathing heavily. "I don't want to hurt you." He released the choke hold, and the father and son walked away.

Although he didn't go around picking fights, Regan made it known at school and in the neighborhood that he wasn't going to take things lying down. When one of Regan's brothers got picked on at his school, Regan came to his defense, delivering a stern warning to the boy who had been bullying his brother. He stepped in to defend a frail classmate and friend named Glen Brausch, whose image as a weakling made him a frequent target of harassment.

"If you were his friend, he was protective of you," Gould recalled. "If you weren't his friend, you were his enemy."

While in high school, Regan got a job unloading and stacking tires at a store near where his father worked. The work was physically demanding but paid a lot more than what he had been making as a newspaper delivery boy. With the money he saved, he bought a used sports car—a Ford Mustang Boss 302—from Cliff Wagner's next-door neighbor. It was golden in color, with black stripes, and although it was more than ten years old, the owner had kept it in great condition.

Overnight, the car earned Regan more admiration and respect from peers than he had ever gotten. Wagner had coveted the car himself, having seen it for years in his neighbor's driveway, and so when Regan came around driving it one day, he was stunned. "I didn't even know it was for sale," Wagner remarked to Regan. His envy was obvious.

It was the first car to be owned by anybody in Regan's circle. Cliff Wagner and other boys in the group would pile into it, and Regan would take them for a drive around the block. On streets with a downward slope, he would idle the engine and take his foot off the brake, letting it roll without hitting the gas pedal. "Step on the gas!" Wagner would yell. "No, it costs too much money," Regan would respond, and they'd keep cruising. No matter how much the others jeered, he knew he was firmly in the driver's seat and didn't have to give up control.

With his poor academic performance, Regan didn't see college in his future. But he didn't want to stay in Farmingdale and work at a factory like his father. He wished to see the world, to travel to some of the exotic locations he'd seen in the James Bond movies. The only way he could think of realizing that ambition was to join the U.S. military.

As a senior in high school, Regan took the Armed Services Vocational Aptitude Battery—a three-hour-long multiple-choice test that the U.S. military has offered to students in the tenth, eleventh, and twelfth grades since 1968. The exam consists of questions for probing an array of basic intellectual skills and knowledge: some questions test for cognitive abilities like pattern recognition and spatial perception; others measure verbal ability; yet others test the exam taker's knowledge of science, social studies, history, and other topics. Depending on the score, applicants have the option of enlisting in the Army, Navy, Air Force, Marines, or Coast Guard. The minimum score required to enter the Air Force, Marines, and Coast Guard is higher than that required to join the Army or the Navy.

Regan appeared for the ASVAB with a number of students at Farmingdale High, including Gould. They took the test in the high school auditorium, scribbling away under the inattentive watch of a bored serviceman proctoring the exam. Regan was seated behind Gould. When the proctor wasn't looking in his direction, he peeked over Gould's shoulder and copied several of the answers. Whatever he lacked in academic ability, he did his best to make up for by taking advantage of his height.

When the results were posted a few months later, he—along

with Gould—was among the high scorers. On his own, he may not have qualified for any of the services. Yet, thanks to the sly peeking he'd been able to get away with, his score was high enough for him to enlist in the Air Force. Regan had done so well, in fact, that he qualified for a job in intelligence, one of the service's more coveted career tracks.

Regan was ecstatic. He'd finally found an escape from Farmingdale. This was his chance to build a new life far away from Lois Lane, leaving behind the painful memories of humiliations and insults he'd suffered there. Since he was still a few months shy of his eighteenth birthday, Anne had to sign a waiver allowing him to enlist. In the summer of 1980, shortly after graduating from Farmingdale High, he packed up his bags and left for Lackland Air Force Base in San Antonio, Texas. Anne wept for days after he said good-bye.

After eight weeks of basic military training at Lackland, Regan went to the Goodfellow Air Force Base in San Angelo, Texas, for technical school. Over the next few months, he learned about signals intelligence and analysis, a cornerstone of modern warfare. It was the most challenging and rigorous academic work he had ever encountered in his life. But Regan was determined to succeed, and he made every effort to overcome whatever impediments his dyslexia posed. As part of his training, he became familiar with Morse code and learned how to detect and intercept radio signals using suitable antennae for specific frequencies and emitting stations. He mastered the basics of interpreting and analyzing these signals to extract intelligence about an enemy.

Graduating from the course, Airman First Class Regan was assigned to a U.S. air station near Iráklion on the Greek island of Crete.

The Air Force had built the facility in 1954 to monitor the Mediterranean, where both the U.S. and the Soviet navies operated their fleets. Spread over a few thousand acres in a rural, idyllic setting, the Iráklion station was equipped with an array of antennas for eavesdropping on military communications throughout the region. Communications between Soviet aircraft and ships were a target of collection, of course. The station was also engaged in intercepting and analyzing signals stemming from the North African and Middle Eastern countries bordering the Mediterranean Sea.

Regan worked with some four hundred signals intelligence analysts who together constituted the 6931st Electronic Security Squad. As he learned the ropes, he came to discover that his dyslexia gave him a unique advantage when it came to doing analysis. Dyslexics tend to think in pictures, not in words, and instead of processing ideas sequentially from the simple to the complex, they are more inclined to look at the big picture. Having a global view helps them make connections between disparate pieces of information and recognize patterns in data that might elude more linear thinkers. As Regan would find out in the course of his assignments, this knack for pattern recognition is a particularly useful thing for a signals analyst to have.

He couldn't have asked for a better first posting. Life on the station was relaxed and enjoyable. The sunny weather was a dreamy contrast to the harsh winters of Farmingdale. The beach was minutes away. For the first time in his life, Regan had a place to call his own, and the privacy that came with it. There were no pesky brothers or sisters to intrude on his space. Within walking distance was a marina where enlisted men and women spent hours swimming and lazing about in paddleboats. Wandering out of the station, one could go picking grapes or visiting ancient Greek ruins. Though the town of Iráklion didn't have much to offer, the big historic metropolis Athens was a ferry ride away.

The charms of Crete had long made it a popular tourist destination for Europeans. During the spring and summer months, thousands of visitors from the west and north of the continent would descend upon the island to enjoy its sandy white beaches and the warm ocean waves that crashed upon them. One day, Regan met a young tourist who was visiting from Sweden. She was blond and blue-eyed and had a shy smile. Her name was Anette Stenqvist.

The two fell in love and kept up a steady correspondence after Anette returned to Sweden. Regan proposed to her in short order. Anette, who had completed only a high school diploma, was happy to shelve her plans of furthering her education in favor of getting married. Regan's prospects seemed bright, and Anette was optimistic about the life she could have in the United States. After Regan completed his Iráklion assignment and took up his next posting at Kelly Air Force Base in San Antonio, Texas, Anette came to the United States to work as an au pair. In March 1983, the two got married.

After two years at Kelly, Regan spent nine months in Korea serving on the Osan Air Base, which the United States had maintained since its intervention in the peninsula during the Korean War. The Air Force routinely conducted reconnaissance flights from the base, flying U-2 spy planes at an altitude of sixty thousand feet above North Korea's territory to photograph military installations and intercept signals of interest. Regan worked with the 6903rd Electronic Security Group, whose primary role was to interpret and analyze the data collected during these missions to produce intelligence reports.

Regan did well in his job, moving up the ranks steadily. His struggles with reading and writing didn't keep him from completing advanced levels of training or clearing the written tests he needed to take to earn promotions. Whether it was by hard work or his talent for visual thinking, he had clearly found a way to compensate.

In the summer of 1985, Regan and Anette moved to Wheeler Air Force Base in Honolulu, Hawaii, where Regan was assigned to work with the 6934th Electronic Security Group. It was a dream posting that would last for the next three years. Regan invited his friend Michael Gould to visit. Gould was impressed by how well Regan was doing, so impressed as to wonder, enviously, if he shouldn't have gone into the military himself.

Regan's apartment on the base was spacious and well furnished. He and Anette seemed to be thriving financially, and they looked happy together. Regan had recently bought a brand-new pickup truck; he and Anette drove Gould around to Honolulu's spectacular beaches. Regan showed off the truck's powerful four-wheel drive, driving the vehicle over the white sands all the way to the shore of Waimea Bay, where the three sunbathed and watched surfers ride the waves under a brilliant blue sky. At night, Regan and his wife took Gould to downtown Honolulu to explore the bars and clubs. Gould returned from the trip thinking that his friend was "stationed on paradise."

Every so often, Regan would visit Farmingdale. Michael and Anne were proud that he had made something of his life, and his brothers and sisters viewed him with a respect and admiration that he hadn't known before. Sometimes, the family would stay up late at night waiting for him to arrive. Anne would make sure to cook him a turkey and a ham, two of Regan's favorite foods. For all the squabbling and fighting of the growing-up years, Regan loved playing big brother to his siblings during these visits, freely dispensing advice. He affectionately chided his younger sister for smoking. "That's no good for you," he told her. "It's going to give you cancer. You should quit." When she asked him what he did in the Air Force, he responded with a cliché of a joke that contained less humor than pride. "I can't tell you," he said. "If I told you, I'd have to kill you."

Once in a while, he'd run into the old gang of tormentors from the neighborhood, including Bob Florio and Cliff Wagner. None of them had left Farmingdale or launched a career, and it must have given Regan some glee to face them in his new avatar as a successful military man doing more for the country than they had ever imagined. One day, when he was hanging out with Florio and Brian Wagner on the lawn of a neighborhood house, he showed off some of the combat maneuvers he had learned in basic training. Florio watched as Regan wrestled Brian Wagner down to the ground with ridiculous ease. Every time the tall and hefty Wagner ended up on his back, Regan let out a laugh. It was all in good fun, but there was one difference from the past. The fun was no longer at his expense.

From Hawaii, Regan was transferred to Washington, D.C., where he attended the NSA's National Cryptologic School for two months of training in signals analysis pertaining specifically to the Middle East and North Africa. Then he began working at the Air Intelligence Agency. He was now a tech sergeant with some management experience under his belt, having supervised a team of analysts in his last two years at Wheeler Air Force Base. For his job at the Air Intelligence Agency (AIA), Regan went beyond analyzing signals to learning how to disrupt an enemy's communication networks.

In August 1990, after Iraqi tanks rolled into Kuwait, the U.S. armed forces began preparing an offensive to drive Iraqi forces from Kuwait's territory. Regan, who had spent part of his career analyzing signal transmissions in the Middle East, was drafted to support the war plans. When, after a buildup of forces, the United States launched Operation Desert Storm on January 16, 1991, Regan worked twelve-hour shifts at the Pentagon to plot—through signals analysis—Iraqi missile sites. He was part of a team that prepared order-of-battle reports on how the Iraqi military planned to deploy their missiles; these reports were used by U.S. commanders to brief the Joint Chiefs of Staff and President George H. W. Bush.

As a communications denial analyst, Regan also had a role to play in jamming communications between Iraqi commanders and their military units, leaving Iraqi fighters with no link to their decision-making nerve centers. By analyzing radar signals and other communications, Regan and analysts with expertise similar to his mapped out the locations of Iraqi air defense systems, including where the Iraqis were positioning their mobile surface-to-air missiles.

For five weeks, a coalition led by the U.S. military carried out a relentless campaign of air strikes over Iraq, bombing military installations and other targets. Saddam Hussein's forces were so weakened by the assault that when U.S. soldiers began a ground offensive on February 24, 1991, it took less than a week to expel the Iraqi army from Kuwait and make an incursion well into Iraq. Only forty-four days after Operation Desert Storm had begun, coalition forces achieved a decisive triumph. There was no doubt that the United States' sophisticated signals intelligence capability, which enabled the coalition to conduct an effective air campaign, had been a key contributor to the relatively easy and resounding victory.

All these years, Regan had helped produce intelligence that fed into strategic decision making and war readiness. Now, for the first time, he had been able to experience the adrenaline rush of contributing to a real-time campaign in which the lives of U.S. soldiers and airmen were at stake. He hadn't been in the heat of battle, but he had played a role in keeping his fellow servicemen and servicewomen safe.

That sense of fulfillment deepened for Regan in the two years that followed, during which time he worked with the Air Force Intelligence Support Agency at the Pentagon. His analysis was now aimed at helping to enforce the two no-fly zones that the U.S.-led coalition had imposed over northern and southern Iraq following Desert Storm, to prevent Iraqi aircraft from bombing the Kurds in the north and Shiite Muslims in the south. Regan's job was to use signals analysis to monitor the mobilization of Iraqi air defense systems, which could threaten coalition aircraft patrolling the no-fly zones and permit the Iraqi air force to make incursions into that space.

Regan's star was on the ascendant. In 1993, he was promoted to master sergeant, and the Air Force awarded him a medal for outstanding leadership. In mid-1994, he was sent to the Joint Military Intelligence College to train for his next job, in an agency that for decades had kept itself completely hidden from the public: the National Reconnaissance Office.

CHAPTER 4

A DESPERATE PLAN

The last thing Francis Gary Powers saw, just before the face shield of his helmet frosted over in the icy atmosphere above the clouds, was the rearview mirror of the U-2 snapping off and flying away. Moments earlier, the thirty-year-old American pilot of the CIA reconnaissance airplane had felt the craft jerk forward as the orange glow of an explosion lit up the cockpit. A missile fired at the U-2 had detonated behind the airplane. Within seconds, Powers knew he had lost control of the craft. Spinning, it plummeted down over the town of Sverdlovsk Oblast near the Ural mountain range in the southwestern Soviet Union.

The day was May 1, 1960. For four years, the U.S. Central Intelligence Agency had been flying reconnaissance missions over the USSR, taking photographs of airfields and missile sites from an altitude of seventy thousand feet—tens of thousands of feet higher than any other type of aircraft could fly. The United States had begun this program of high-altitude spying after the Soviet leader Nikita

Khrushchev rejected President Dwight Eisenhower's proposal for an "open skies" treaty, under which the United States and the USSR would have given each other permission to conduct aerial surveillance of each other's military installations to verify that the two countries were complying with arms control agreements. Although the Soviet Union knew about the overflight program, the CIA was positive that Soviet radar couldn't track the movement of the U-2s. In what constituted further assurance for the United States, the highest-known altitude that the best Soviet interceptor, the MiG-17 fighter aircraft, could reach was forty-five thousand feet.

The May 1 overflight, named Operation Grand Slam, was the most ambitious reconnaissance mission to have been planned since the U-2 program began. Unlike the twenty-three missions that had been flown before, all of which had entered and exited Soviet airspace from the same direction, this one was to traverse the length of the country from its southern border to the northwest. Powers took off from an Air Force base in Peshawar, Pakistan, and flew northwest, crossing Afghanistan to enter the USSR, flying on toward Tyuratam, just east of the Aral Sea, and then onward to the Ural Mountains. From there, he was to take a sharp left turn toward Kirov and then head north again, flying over Severodvinsk and Murmansk before landing in Bodø, Norway.

But now, four and a half hours into the flight, Powers was in rapid descent, having ejected himself from the U-2 after its dismemberment by the missile strike. Contrary to what the Americans had believed, Soviet radar had, in fact, been able to track the airplane successfully. When Powers had come down to below an altitude of fifteen thousand feet, his parachute unfurled above him, yanking his body up as it halted his fall. Drifting down, he pulled out a map from his pocket, tore it up into tiny pieces, and scattered it like confetti—destroying any evidence that might reveal that he was on an intelligence-gathering mission.

Powers gazed down at the picturesque Russian countryside below, its hills and forests and roads and buildings growing sharper in definition with his descent. He pulled out a silver dollar that the CIA had given to him and all U-2 pilots to carry on missions. It wasn't really a dollar but a carrying case for a pin laced with curare—a suicide device to be used in dire circumstances. Worried that a shiny dollar would be a tempting souvenir for his Russian captors, Powers unscrewed the metal loop at the end of it, took out the pin—which was covered in a sheath—and slipped it into his pocket before throwing the dollar away.

He considered whether to use the poison pin as a way of ending the uncertainty that lay before him. But hopeful that he might escape, he dismissed the idea.

What awaited Powers was a two-year ordeal that he would later recount in *Operation Overflight: A Memoir of the U-2 Incident*. After landing in a plowed field, he was handed over to the authorities and thrown in jail. The U.S. government, assuming that Powers had died in a crash, issued a cover story about one of its weather planes having gone off course. But the pieces of the U-2, along with much of the reconnaissance equipment it was carrying, had been recovered by the Soviets, and Khrushchev took delight in disproving the United States' claim to the world days later.

On August 17, 1960, a Soviet court convicted Powers on charges of espionage and handed down a ten-year sentence. Luckily for Powers, his jail term was cut short by a prisoner exchange in 1962 between the two superpowers. Powers and another American imprisoned in the USSR were released in exchange for a Soviet spy who had been sentenced in the United States.

The downing of the U-2 and the capture of Powers forced the CIA to stop overflights of the Soviet Union. Yet America's need for continued aerial surveillance over the vast territory of its Cold War rival was even greater on account of the Soviet Union's successful 1957 launch of *Sputnik 1*. Not only had the launch demonstrated the Soviets' technological edge over the United States; it had also raised fears that the USSR might be able to aim nuclear warheads at the continental United States, using the same rocket that had catapulted *Sputnik 1* into orbit. Consequently, it was vital for the United States to find an alternate way of gathering intelligence about the USSR's military capabilities and preparedness.

The Eisenhower administration had been quietly working on a solution that some officials saw as overly ambitious and perhaps impractical: the ability to conduct surveillance from space. The capture of Francis Gary Powers gave an added impetus to the effort. By the time Powers returned home in February 1962, the United States had become adept at deploying spy satellites in orbit for the purposes of reconnaissance. The capability would give the United States an unprecedented strategic and military advantage over its adversaries in the years to come.

When the U.S. government conceived of its program of satellite photoreconnaissance—code-named Corona—in the late fifties, the concept seemed outlandish. A satellite carrying a camera would be blasted into orbit about a hundred miles above Earth. After it took pictures, the satellite would release a capsule carrying the exposed film. The capsule, or film bucket, would fall back toward Earth, protected by a heat shield to guard against the high temperatures it would be subjected to upon reentry into the atmosphere. At about eleven miles from Earth, the heat shield would be cast off and a parachute would deploy, allowing the capsule to be snagged in midair by an airplane.

The challenge of accomplishing this feat was driven home by a string of failures starting in 1959. There were twelve attempts that proved unsuccessful, either because the rocket misfired on the launchpad, or the satellite couldn't be placed into orbit, or the camera failed to operate, or the reentry capsule was ejected prematurely and couldn't be retrieved.

The thirteenth try, made on August 10, 1960, worked like a charm. The satellite went into orbit as planned, the capsule was released at the right time, and the parachute deployed as it was supposed to. The capsule was recovered from the Pacific Ocean. This was, however, a test launch, with no film involved. Just eight days later, the next satellite was fired into space bearing a capsule containing three thousand feet of film. After ejection and reentry into the atmosphere, when it was on its way down toward the Pacific, an airplane flying out of Hickam Air Force Base in Hawaii plucked it out of the air on its third attempt. On August 25, scientists and engineers gathered in the Oval Office to show Eisenhower the results of the country's first successful satellite photoreconnaissance mission. The film had captured 1.65 million square miles of Soviet territory—more than the area covered by all the U-2 missions over the USSR combined.

A new agency was created within the Department of Defense to manage space-based intelligence collection: the National Reconnaissance Office. The American public knew about the newly created National Aeronautics and Space Administration, but the existence of the NRO—entrusted with running what was in effect a secret space program—would remain hidden for decades.

Over the next twelve years, another 144 satellites were launched under Corona. Even though the imagery acquired by the camera systems they were equipped with steadily improved in resolution, going from between fifty to thirty-five feet to under ten feet, the U.S. intelligence community realized that it needed a sharper imaging capability to get detailed information about specific military sites. That led to the development of a new camera capable of photographing defined targets such as a single missile base. The first such camera was launched into orbit in 1963 aboard a satellite code-named Gambit. Another thirty-seven Gambit launches followed over the next four years. While Corona's mission was to bring back panoramic views that could be searched for military installations, the Gambit satellites were deployed to take follow-up pictures of sites identified with the help of imagery acquired through Corona.

Behind these satellites and cameras were not just billions of dollars in government investment but also the best that American ingenuity and innovation had to offer. Aside from developing a film capsule that could survive reentry and devising the precise controls necessary to have the capsule land where desired, researchers spent years refining the camera systems so that they could function flawlessly in the vacuum conditions of space. For the missions, Eastman Kodak made a special film with three times the resolution of the best aerial photography ever done before. When the acetate-based film showed a tendency to break in space, the company switched to a polyester-based film, which also decreased the film's thickness significantly and enabled later missions to fly with twice as much film as the early ones.

There was an especially intense effort to improve the sharpness of photographs taken by the Gambit satellites, for any detailed analysis of the Soviet arsenal depended on them. To test the upgrades made to the cameras, the NRO had retirees from the military drive out to farms across the United States and lay down canvas sheets in the middle of open fields, upon which bars were placed at varying distances from one another. The satellite photos of these targets, showing how far apart the bars had to be to be distinguishable, were a way to measure improvements. Through incremental advances and occasional leaps, these "close-look" satellites were eventually able to return photographs with a resolution of less than six inches—good enough for analysts to study even small changes in the design of Soviet tanks.

Unbeknownst to ordinary Americans, the photoreconnaissance from Corona and Gambit quickly became indispensable to U.S. intelligence gathering. The film buckets retrieved from the satellites over the Pacific Ocean were flown by a high-speed jet to a classified facility on the East Coast where the film was processed. In the early days, copies of the photographs were physically sent to intelligence agencies throughout the government, from the Defense Intelligence Agency to the CIA to intelligence divisions of the Army, Navy, and Air Force. In later years, the film began to be scanned and transmitted electronically.

Gathering photographic intelligence wasn't the only endeavor of the national reconnaissance program. In parallel with the imaging satellites, the United States also sent up satellites to collect signals intelligence, starting with one launched in 1960 under the cover "Galactic Radiation and Background." True to its name, GRAB had a publicly acknowledged scientific purpose—that of measuring radiation in space—but it was also equipped with antennas and other instruments to eavesdrop on electromagnetic transmissions from Soviet air defense systems. GRAB-1 and its successor satellites recorded these signals on tape; the information was then downloaded remotely at radio receiving units on the ground. By analyzing the signals, the U.S. military was able to locate and characterize Soviet radar installations and develop plans for air strikes in the event of a war.

Preparing for conflict may have been a key objective of the United States' reconnaissance program, but its biggest contribution during the Cold War was to help prevent the escalation of hostilities between the United States and the Soviet Union. Imagery obtained by Corona satellites in the early sixties showed that the Soviet Union had a far smaller arsenal of long-range missiles than the U.S. government had previously thought. Through the following two decades, satellite intelligence allowed U.S. policy makers and strategic planners to accurately estimate the number of missiles, bombers, and submarines the Soviet Union held. The Soviets had their own reconnaissance satellites, which similarly helped allay their fears about the United States' capabilities and intent. When the USSR and the United States signed a strategic arms control treaty in 1971, accepting limits on the number of missiles they could maintain, they relied on their spy satellites to monitor the agreements.

The role of reconnaissance in helping ease tensions on either side during this era was perhaps best articulated by a Russian intelligence official named Georgiy Polischuk years later, in 1996, when he came to Washington for discussions between U.S. and Russian officials on using satellite imagery for environmental monitoring. Both the American and the Russian delegations at the meeting had representatives who had worked in the field of space-based reconnaissance on behalf of their respective governments. Prior to the breakup of the Soviet Union, Polischuk had headed the Soviet counterpart to the NRO. "I am proud of my service and of yours," he said at the meeting, speaking to an audience that included an ex-director of the NRO, Marty Faga. "We both labored during the Cold War to keep our leaders informed. Every time our leaders feared the worst, our hard evidence showed that the intentions of the other side were not so dire. I know that we both helped prevent the Cold War from becoming a hot one."

Through all those years, however, the United States never acknowledged the existence of the NRO, even though President Jimmy Carter hinted at it in a 1978 speech on U.S. accomplishments in space, remarking that "photoreconnaissance satellites have become an important stabilizing factor in world affairs in the monitoring of arms control agreements." Despite that pronouncement, which was the first statement to Americans that satellites were being used to collect intelligence, the NRO remained an entirely "black" organization operating out of a hallway of offices in the Pentagon that lay behind a set of double doors marked 4C-956.

This official veil of secrecy—maintained primarily out of concern that other countries might object to being surveilled from space—didn't protect the NRO from losing its secrets, however. In the mid-seventies, a young defense contractor named Christopher Boyce, working with his boyhood friend Andrew Daulton Lee, passed on to Soviet officials documents containing classified information about the development of U.S. spy satellites. In 1977, shortly after the two were convicted, a low-ranking CIA clerk named William Kampiles stole the manual of the KH-11 spy satellite and sold it to officials at the Soviet embassy in Athens for a mere $3,000. He was sentenced to forty years in prison but released after serving nineteen years.

Unlike its predecessor satellites, the KH-11 was capable of

transmitting imagery in the form of signals to ground stations rather than dropping film canisters out of space. As the technology for relaying photographic data to Earth advanced through the eighties, U.S. intelligence officials were able to get images of targets in close to real time. The advantage this offered went beyond strategic decision making—the military could now use satellite intelligence tactically, in the conduct of operations on the battlefield.

The difference that this type of intelligence could make was evident in 1991 during the First Gulf War. The real-time availability of photoreconnaissance—combined with signals intelligence collected by satellites as well as ground stations—enabled U.S. commanders to anticipate and counter various Iraqi offensives with an ease that even the most optimistic military planners couldn't have expected. Where U.S. combat forces could have suffered hundreds of casualties, they lost relatively few soldiers, and the U.S.-led coalition won a swift victory in less than seven weeks of operations.

Despite the success, Pentagon officials realized that the tactical advantage conferred by the satellites hadn't been fully utilized. They identified a host of problems with how the intelligence had been pushed out to the field. There were times when the imagery was "late, unsatisfactory or unusable," a House Armed Services Committee found. While the war had demonstrated the usefulness of the spy satellites in supporting combat operations, it had also underscored the imperative for the reconnaissance program to quickly deliver specific intelligence requested by war fighters on the ground.

It was against this backdrop that the then director of the agency, Marty Faga, recommended that the government make the NRO's existence public. That the United States had a reconnaissance program was by now an open secret. Many other countries were known to have their own spy satellites in space, which lessened the weight of any international objections. Faga made the argument that it would be hard to disseminate the NRO's intelligence products widely and effectively within the military if the NRO continued to stay in the shadows.

The government agreed to lift the veil, and on September 18, 1992, the Defense Department issued a quiet memorandum declassifying the NRO and naming its top three officials, including Faga. At an all-hands meeting at the agency, Faga told employees the rationale behind the declassification. At the end of the meeting, an employee came up to him with a question.

"So now can we have coffee cups with the NRO logo?" she asked.

"Well, yeah," Faga replied. By 1995, after the agency had moved into its spanking-new headquarters in Chantilly, it had its own souvenir shop offering golf balls, coasters, and mugs bearing the NRO insignia.

Brian Regan came to the NRO in 1995 as the organization, responding to pressure from Congress and the Pentagon, was in the middle of ramping up its tactical support to the military. Regan was assigned to an office responsible for helping military units in the field access and utilize intelligence collected by spy satellites. His primary job was to support training exercises in which soldiers and their command structures are put in battle-like situations similar to what they might encounter in an actual war.

The U.S. military conducts these exercises not just on U.S. soil but also in other parts of the world where it has a military presence. The aim is to keep soldiers and commanders and the entire war machine ever ready to engage in conflict anywhere in the world.

Making the simulations realistic is key to the quality of the training. The military devotes considerable resources to creating mock theaters of battle to mimic conflict zones that U.S. soldiers expect to fight in, for instance, re-creating Afghan villages—complete with mosques and shops and hired Afghan men—in the middle of California's Mojave Desert.

The exercises include ground offensives as well as air campaigns flown against air defense systems that mimic those used by adversaries. In the mock battle theaters where such campaigns are conducted, pilots must contend with radar and antiaircraft artillery and surface-to-air missiles deployed against them, just as they would in enemy territory.

Regan's role in these exercises was to help set up the air defenses pilots had to train against. He had to draw upon his knowledge of how countries like Iraq and Libya deployed their radar and antiaircraft weaponry, and recommend where all of that equipment needed to be positioned in a replicated battle zone. He helped write scripts for how these defenses would work in an exercise, how they would communicate with one another, and how they would attempt to conceal themselves to deceive U.S. commanders and pilots. It was part of his job to think like an enemy.

Regan also helped train pilots and ground fighters to monitor these defenses by accessing signals intelligence gleaned from their emissions by NRO satellites. For instance, if a surface-to-air missile were moved from one location to another during an exercise, the war fighter had to be able to discern that movement from signals picked up by satellite reconnaissance. Another part of Regan's job was to go out to where the defense systems had been deployed and determine their geocoordinates using a GPS, as well as ascertain other characteristics of their operations, such as when a radar was turned on and turned off. By comparing information collected on the ground to similar information derived through observations from space, the NRO was able to test the accuracy and timeliness of its signals intelligence data.

Being assigned to the NRO was a blessing for Regan, who might otherwise have had to move out of Washington, D.C., for his next posting in the Air Force. By 1995, he and Anette had already spent seven years in the D.C. area, the longest they had lived anywhere. They had bought a small town house in Bowie, Maryland, a place to finally call home. Regan was glad not to have to pack up and settle in a new town, as men and women in the military must do every few years.

The couple now had three children—two little girls and a boy. Raising them was more than a full-time job for Anette, especially since Regan was often out traveling to the venues of military exercises within the United States and abroad. He had to drive forty miles to get to his office in Chantilly, a joyless commute that took him an hour and a half each way, making him unavailable to lend Anette much of a helping hand. The carefree existence the two had known in Hawaii was a thing of the past, replaced by the stresses of parenting.

Regan had never been one to socialize with neighbors or colleagues, and as he got older, he became increasingly reclusive. At the NRO, where he shared an office with three others, he wore earplugs to block out noise, including coworkers' conversations. During meetings in which he and other enlisted staffers like him had to take orders from commissioned officers—usually younger and better paid—Regan often wore an unsmiling expression that exuded resentment. He visited the vending machine periodically to buy cans of Mountain Dew, guzzling large volumes of the soda at his desk through the day. Perhaps in part because of all the sugar he was consuming, Regan acquired a bulging midriff, which made him stand out among his mostly trim coworkers.

Regan's job, too, set him apart from colleagues in his unit, known as the Performance and Evaluation division. While his role was to set up exercises and collect field data, most of his coworkers were assigned to higher-order tasks that were more intellectually demanding: assessing the quality of the signals intelligence gathered, writing reports on the performance of the NRO systems, making recommendations to improve them. The division was staffed by some of the brightest men and women from the enlisted ranks, and Regan, who had fought an uphill battle since childhood to prove his intellectual mettle, couldn't help feeling inadequate in their midst. Since the nature of his work was different from what the others did, Regan's presentations were quickly dispensed with in staff meetings, so that the group could move on to more interesting things. As a coworker would later recall: "It was almost like—OK, Brian, just make sure you are doing your thing and being productive. The rest of us were involved in doing more cutting-edge stuff."

Regan may have been able to brush off the dismissive vibe he experienced in these interactions if he hadn't suffered other insults. As had been the case in his middle and high school years, his odd personality made him a butt of jokes within the group. Some coworkers made fun of him, not quite good-naturedly, for being overweight. It didn't help that he wasn't as sharply dressed as them, or that his desk was always an untidy mess, or that his car frequently broke down on his commute to work. The impression that took hold was that Regan wasn't competent to manage his daily life in the way that a responsible adult should be able to.

More than his appearance, it was the situations Regan got into that invited gibes from some in the group, especially from a coworker named Ken Jackman, who may have been Regan's biggest tormentor. Not long after Regan's fourth child was born, he accidentally dropped the infant boy on his head. When he shared the incident with co-workers, Jackman—whose low opinion of Regan's intelligence was no secret around the office—turned the story into a running joke. On another occasion, Regan's coworkers were amused that he spent days trying to guess the four-digit code needed to make his car radio work. The easier option would have been to go to an automobile dealership, but Regan didn't want to pay. That he could crack the code if he just kept trying, and that the few bucks he'd save was worth this much effort: both seemed like foolish convictions to the others. It was the kind of behavior that, in the words of one coworker, made people chuckle and say, "I can't believe Brian's doing that again."

Being held in low esteem by peers—no matter how jovial the banter—was a depressingly familiar situation for Regan, a throwback to life as a kid in Farmingdale. In the years since, he had learned not to shrink away from barbs, to stand his ground and reclaim respect through any means possible. At the NRO, he responded to the teasing and humiliation with a defiance he had cultivated since high school. Every now and then, he would come out of his shell of introversion to brag about his knowledge of the financial market and to advise coworkers on what stocks to buy. His claim of being a wise investor poised for big gains in the market struck his colleagues as oddly discordant with his shabby clothes, his barely drivable car, and his penchant for thrift. When members of the group were about to travel to another city for work, he boastfully claimed to know which hotel would be the best for them to stay at. His coworkers found out later that the advice wasn't based on his own experience, as he had been pretending, but was borrowed from someone else.

To boost his status in the outside world, he came up with the idea of using a fake CIA placard in his car. He created it by taking a printout of the CIA emblem and pasting it on a piece of cardboard, along with the words: "On Official Business." He would often take the placard with him on his travels around the United States and put it up on the windshield when going out to restaurants and bars, aiming to impress women he hoped to meet, as well as lower his chances of getting a parking ticket. There was something comical about these shallow attempts to inflate his importance, and it didn't exactly build the respect he was seeking. "We would joke about how he thought he had the right answers to everything, and he didn't," a coworker would later recall.

Regan strived, in more earnest ways, to improve his self-image and social standing. He worked out at the gym in the basement of his office building, hoping to shed some pounds. He had never developed a reading habit because of his dyslexia, and the resulting lack of erudition bothered him. To compensate, he borrowed audiobooks from the library to teach himself history, sociology, and other subjects. He suspected, rightly, that others saw him as unsophisticated, and he believed he could change that by walking his own path of self-development.

Yet navigating everyday life itself was a challenge for Regan. Like many other dyslexics, he was in the habit of making lists to get things done. Written on index cards and sheets of paper, hundreds of such lists lay strewn all over his house and in his car, mirroring the chaos they were intended to manage. Some contained tasks to be done at the office: "Clear off desk, pass on duty to other." Others were detailed checklists in preparation for a trip: "Lock doors, electric off, towels, underwear, undershirt, snacks, drinks, Vodka bottle." Some read like self-motivational scripts: "Education, Read, Go to school,

Follow it step by step, Every day do a little studying towards your goal." He jotted down aphorisms—"Repetition is the mother of skill"—and notes to remind himself of priorities: "Spend more time with family." On his day-to-day lists, he sometimes included mindless instructions that seemed scripted by, and for, an automaton: "Get up." "Take the bus to work." "Shower." "Change clothes."

Perhaps these jottings were clues to the tragic dysfunction of a man isolated and unmoored from the world. Regan seemed to be alone, not just at his job but also in his personal life. His relationship with Anette had been fraying for years. The pressure of raising four children, one of them a newborn, had put a severe strain on the couple. The marriage wasn't loveless, but it was in choppy waters.

Anette had once dreamed of becoming a Hollywood star, of living a life of luxury. She loved horseback riding, which she dabbled in at considerable expense, and wanted to own a horse ranch someday. But after nearly a decade and a half with Regan, she could see her dreams crumbling. It made her hard and bitter. A neat and organized person by nature, she hated Regan's habit of visiting thrift stores to buy collectible items—McDonald's toys, figurines, Barbie dolls. He thought they would be valuable one day. It drove her crazy that he hoarded them in the basement of their cramped house, along with the comics and toys and baseball cards he'd collected since childhood. She grumbled about it to neighbors.

The day's grind left her with little energy at the end of the day to connect with Regan, who would call her before leaving work to ask, in a predictably expressionless monotone, what she had made for dinner. When one of her neighbors was going through a divorce, Anette told her: "Be happy you are alone, because if you love somebody, you don't know what you'll get. Love is a crapshoot."

Regan made halfhearted attempts to revive the relationship. Every now and then, especially before flying off on work trips, he would write reminders to himself to bring her flowers or write her a love note. But when traveling, he wasn't always a faithful husband and was known to look for one-night stands on Craigslist. Once, on a trip to Farmingdale by himself to visit family, he picked up a girl from a bar after an evening out with Michael Gould. In 2001, when the FBI was surveilling him, agents observed him drive up to a woman who was walking down the street, lower his car window, and proposition her. His lack of finesse was equally on display at the beach, where surveillance agents watched him unabashedly ogle women.

Most summers, Anette took the kids to Sweden. Despite traveling part of the way on military flights—a benefit granted to Air Force personnel and their dependents—the trips cost thousands of dollars that Regan could ill afford. With a take-home income of less than $40,000 a year, he was already in dire financial straits. By the late nineties, he had more than a dozen credit cards in his name, with unpaid balances in the tens of thousands of dollars. On stickers on the faces of the cards, he wrote down how much credit he had left on each and used money from one card to make payments on another. A smarter choice, instead of this accounting jugglery, might have been to stop going out all the time to eat lunch at Don Pablo's or Talkin Turkey, a habit that helped neither his wallet nor his paunch. But Regan did little to check Anette's spending or his own, sinking deeper and deeper into the hole.

If there was one thing Regan prided himself on, it was his resourcefulness. He believed he was inventive, even though the ideas he thought up sometimes ended up as epic failures. In the early nineties, when he and Anette lived on Bolling Air Force Base in Washington, D.C., he began riding his bike to the Pentagon to try to keep himself in shape. He didn't want to show up for work in sweaty clothes; he decided that he needed to carry his uniform with him on the bike every morning and change when he got in. He built a suit rack for the bicycle—a metal frame bolted onto the back that he could hang his uniform on. When he rode the rigged-up bike, however, he realized that the hanging suit was a sail that slowed him down considerably as it billowed out behind him in the breeze. Once, as he was riding over the Fourteenth Street Bridge, the effect was strong enough to make the bike wobble until Regan lost control of it and fell sideways onto a grassy patch at the end of the bike path.

Such debacles didn't stop Regan from continuing to believe that he had a knack for clever solutions, no matter how intractable the problem. In the face of his worsening financial situation—his credit card debt had crossed $47,000 by the end of 1998—he nurtured dreams of becoming rich overnight. Time and again, he traveled to Las Vegas to try his luck at the casinos, succeeding only in blowing away money. He thought he could make a fortune by playing the stock market. He'd picked up the basics of how to analyze stocks from consulting books and popular articles, and although the resulting knowledge was rudimentary, he sought to apply it by engaging in online stock trading from his desktop at the NRO. The results of this gambling, as in Las Vegas, did not go in his favor.

Regan's unshakable belief that he possessed deep insights into how markets work wasn't his only delusion. He also came up with harebrained inventions that he thought could make him a load of cash. One was a concept for a baby-bottle dryer—a plastic stand with spokes on which to put empty bottles to dry. He sent his design, along with a fee, to a company that claimed to market innovative ideas. In due course, he realized, much to his dismay, that the company was more interested in cashing his check than in promoting what he had imagined to be a million-dollar idea.

Regan didn't share the sorry state of his finances with anybody, not even his parents and siblings back in Farmingdale. Regan had grown up in the shadow of a father who preferred to drink away his troubles rather than discuss them, so Regan's reluctance to ask for help wasn't surprising. Perhaps he worried about losing the respect he'd struggled so hard to win from his birth family. In any case, he had been more successful, careerwise, than anybody else in the family: who could he really turn to for financial support? On visits to Farmingdale with Anette and their kids, he showed no signs of the stress he was under because of his mounting debt. He joked and cackled with his brothers and sisters as he'd always done. He took Anette and the children to enjoy the beaches of Long Island that he'd visited so often when growing up. He went shopping with them for toys and clothes. During these brief stays at Lois Lane, he helped fix his parents' washing machine and did other handy jobs around the house. He wanted to be seen as a problem solver who could be relied on, not as someone who had no solutions to problems of his own.

Yet, as the gap between Regan's debt and his income widened, he became increasingly worried about the future. Anette had begun taking classes at Prince George's Community College to meet the prerequisites for entering a nursing program there, but it was going to take a few years for her to become a nurse. For now, the classes were simply adding to the family's debt burden. There didn't seem to be any relief in sight. Regan was so desperate to get away from it all that there were times when he would leave home, telling

Anette that he had to travel for work, check into a motel room, and binge-drink for an entire weekend.

One day, he sat down with Anette and suggested they file for bankruptcy. Although she knew enough about their finances to understand that they could no longer get by on a single income, she had been oblivious to how dire the situation was. Regan hadn't given her any warnings earlier, and his suggestion struck her like a bolt from the blue. But rather than recognize that drastic measures were needed to avert financial doom, she chose to worry about the social stigma the family would suffer if they declared bankruptcy. Her answer was a firm no.

Regan didn't press her. What he needed now, more than ever, was a plan that would make him rich in a short span of time.

On a pleasant summer evening in 1999, Regan drove to Michael Gould's house in Farmingdale. He was in town for a few days visiting his parents. Anette and the kids hadn't come with him on the trip, and Regan wanted to make the most of his stay. In earlier years, when he and Gould used to go clubbing, he would show up at Gould's house with a bottle of vodka bought from the liquor store so that the two could drink on the way to nightclubs rather than have to buy expensive drinks once they got there. On this evening, though, the two headed to a bar.

They stayed there for several hours, knocking back vodka shots and beers and reminiscing about the old days—the movies they'd watched together at the Sunrise multiplex, the experience of delivering newspapers, the good times they had shared in Hawaii. They could have spent all night drinking and talking, but a little past one a.m., with not much time to go before the bar's closing, the two got in the car and drove back to the neighborhood. Regan pulled up next to Gould's house. The two sat in the parked car and continued to talk, as they drank some more beers.

It was a beautiful night. Regan had rolled down the car's windows, letting in the breeze. The conversation turned to Glen Brausch, the classmate whom Regan had once protected from bullying in middle school. Brausch had died young, not long after his bar mitzvah, at the age of sixteen. Regan remarked how sad it was that Brausch never got the chance to grow up and see the world.

"Well, at least he's in a better place now," Gould said, hoping that Regan would find solace in his words.

Regan turned to him with a stoic gaze.

"I don't believe in the afterlife," he said. "I don't believe in God."

Gould was taken aback, both by Regan's statement and by the absoluteness with which he had made it. He knew Regan's parents to be devout Catholics. He knew they had given Regan and his brothers and sisters a religious upbringing, making sure to take them to church. Regan had never before said anything to Gould suggesting that he wasn't a man of faith. To learn that Regan had somehow turned into a nonbeliever was troubling to Gould, who was Jewish.

"But don't you believe in heaven and hell?" he asked.

"I don't," Regan said. There was a finality to his tone that suggested he had given the question a fair amount of thought before arriving at his stance.

Gould attempted to persuade him. "I think that's a very morbid thing to think, that there's no afterlife," he told Regan. "To think that there are no consequences for your actions."

It was evident to Regan that his friend felt disappointed and hurt. But he was unmoved. He cared only about this existence, he told Gould, because in his mind, there was nothing beyond it.

"You only get a onetime shot at life, and that's it."

Gould didn't give up. "Listen, you really should try to change your position if you don't want a broken path," he said before getting out of the car and saying good night. As Regan drove off, the sound of his car fading into the night, Gould had the disturbing thought that his friend was perhaps losing his moral compass. Little did he know that Regan was about to walk down a treacherous path—one that led to treason.

The idea of committing espionage began taking shape in Regan's mind through the early months of 1999 as he found himself in the vortex of a perfect storm created by the continuing humiliations at work, the worsening of his financial situation, and the growing rift in his marriage. From the average evaluations he had been getting, he knew he wasn't going to be promoted anytime soon. The Air Force wanted to transfer him to Europe, but Regan wasn't willing to move because of the disruption it would cause his family. When the Air Force turned down his request to defer overseas deployment, he had to choose between accepting the transfer and retiring a year later, on August 31, 2000, when he would complete twenty years of service. Grudgingly, he opted for the latter.

With the clock ticking toward retirement, Regan's anxieties about the future transformed into a rising sense of panic. Because of the narrow scope of the work he'd been doing at the NRO, he wasn't sure he would be able to find a well-paying job in industry, certainly not with the ease that his coworkers expected to. Clutching at straws, Regan finally saw a way out of this insecurity.

He would cash in on the nation's secrets.

Growing up, he had learned that getting what he wanted sometimes meant having to break the rules. He hadn't experienced any negative consequences for having stolen the ceramic art tools from his neighbor's house, or for cheating on his military entrance test. Those might have been small misdemeanors, but the principle he'd taken away from them applied equally to the crime he was now planning to commit.

All that mattered was not getting caught. As long as he could get away with it, espionage was a legitimate answer to his troubles.

It was also one that seemed to lie within easy grasp. One of Regan's secondary responsibilities at his job was to help maintain his division's Web page on Intelink, the intranet of the U.S. intelligence community and a platform for the sharing and dissemination of information among the country's various intelligence agencies. In doing that part of his job, Regan had become keenly familiar with Intelink and what it held. Resident on the intranet's thousands of Web pages and databases, he knew, was an array of secrets the United States had spent billions to acquire, from reports of intelligence gathered by American spies around the world to analyses of images and signals captured through reconnaissance. The way Regan came to see it, Intelink was the doorway to a basement stuffed with treasures waiting to be sold to enemies of the United States.

Regan began exploring the depth and breadth of Intelink, browsing content that went far beyond his assigned responsibilities. To do his job as an exercise agent, he mostly needed to access pages relating to signals intelligence, as well as air defenses in the Middle East and North Africa. But through the fall and winter months,

Regan accessed a diverse selection of images and intelligence reports—a profile of a Libyan general, the United States' capabilities for destroying military sites hidden deep underground, an adversary's handbook for conducting biological warfare. His surfing sessions became longer and more frequent. By early 2001, he was spending hours on Intelink every week.

Regan devoted part of his surfing to educating himself about espionage. He searched Intelink for reports by analysts on how spies through U.S. history had committed their acts of betrayal—how these men and women went about stealing secrets and transferring them to other governments, how they were discovered and investigated, and how they were brought to justice. While researching this literature, Regan learned about a counterintelligence course that he was eligible to take as a member of the intelligence community. His supervisor didn't ask any questions when he requested approval to attend the course, for even though Regan's job had nothing to do with counterintelligence, learning about it could help him become more alert to potential espionage in his environment, making him a better sentinel of the nation's secrets. And so, for a few days in late 1999, Regan took time out of his job at the NRO to attend classes at Tysons Corner, Virginia, where he heard former FBI and CIA agents present espionage case studies.

By learning about these cases in detail, Regan hoped to gain insights that would help him craft his own plans. He wished to avoid the mistakes that traitors before him had made. With sufficient foresight and planning, he told himself, he would pull off the perfect espionage conspiracy. Unbeknownst to all those coworkers and classmates who had ever doubted his intelligence, he would transform himself into the ultimate spy.

Starting in the fall of 1999, Regan's visits to the printer at his office grew increasingly frequent. He was printing out hundreds of pages of classified information from Intelink. He would first compile the information digitally, on his desktop, using a program called Snagit that allowed him to copy several pages into one file. He could then print out a large set of pages with a single command, saving himself the trouble of walking back and forth to the printer too many times.

In his four years at the NRO, Regan had never been a heavy user of the printer. If his coworkers had paid any attention, they would have wondered why he was collecting printouts with such regularity. But luckily for Regan, nobody noticed.

As he began accumulating these documents, Regan thought carefully about the next steps in his plan. Most U.S. spies who had betrayed the country were tasked by a foreign government to steal and pass information, but Regan had initiated his espionage scheme on his own, with no prior relationship with intelligence agents of another country. Unlike earlier turncoats like the CIA's Aldrich Ames and James Nicholson, who served as U.S. spies for decades before selling out to an adversary, Regan had no experience or knowledge of how to operate in this shadowy world. He had never targeted foreign intelligence officers for recruitment, as Ames and Nicholson had done in the course of their work as CIA agents. He was going to have to devise his own way of contacting a foreign service and marketing the information he was gathering.

What countries could he target? From all the research he had done, Regan had drawn one key conclusion. He wasn't going to engage with Russian intelligence. For in some instances, Regan had learned, Russian agents who had defected to the United States had ended up disclosing the identities of American moles working for the Russians. Regan wasn't willing to take that risk.

He turned his sights to the Middle East and North Africa, a part of the world he'd concentrated on during much of his career. In the decade since the end of the Cold War, the region had become a focus of increasing attention for U.S. military planners. Following the collapse of the Soviet Union, the United States no longer had a single rival superpower to worry about. Instead, it had to contend with a growing military challenge from China, an emerging power, and a host of smaller adversaries, many of them oil-rich countries with a majority Muslim population: Iraq, Libya, Iran, Sudan. Each of these nations, Regan thought, would be willing to pay for secrets that might help them militarily against the United States.

Regan tailored his explorations on Intelink accordingly. He collected images and reports on China that could help the Chinese military understand precisely how much the United States knew about the country's nuclear installations, missile systems, and other strategic sites. He entered "top secret iran" into the intranet's search engine and sifted through the results. He cast another wide net by searching for "top secret libya," misspelling "Libya" on more than one occasion. He looked for material that would be valuable to the Iraqi regime, whose long-standing conflict with the United States was escalating toward the possibility of another full-scale war. Regan didn't just gather information that would help the countries he had in mind—Libya, Iraq, and Iran among them—in hostilities against the United States. He also downloaded whatever intelligence he could find on the military capabilities of regional neighbors like Israel, which he expected his target countries would be equally interested in.

Regan couldn't simply stack this growing volume of printouts on his desk. He stored them in a credenza that sat between his cubicle and his neighbor's. Every now and then, he would open it, add a new bundle of documents to the holdings, and lock it up again. Nobody asked him any questions.

The storage proved to be more secure than he could have imagined. Once, when Regan was traveling on assignment, members of the NRO's building management staff came by his office looking to pick up unused furniture. Nobody spoke up for the credenza, and so they took it away. Later, when they discovered that it was locked, they used a drill to unlock it. Inside they found hundreds of documents.

When Regan returned, one of them called him to ask if the papers belonged to him. He replied in the affirmative, trying to stay calm despite feeling a wave of worry about being found out. The staff wrapped up the documents and sent them all back to him. Whether by sheer good fortune or because of complete obliviousness on the part of the NRO's management, Regan had dodged a major bullet. Relieved, he stuffed the printouts in an overhead cabinet, which felt like a safer storage space than the credenza, even if only because it was affixed to the wall.

One day in March 2000, Regan pulled out a sheaf of documents from his stash and placed it at the bottom of his gym bag. His sweaty workout clothes lay on top of the papers in a disheveled heap. At around five p.m., he logged out of his computer, picked up the bag, and walked out of his cubicle toward the building exit.

His heart was racing, but Regan walked unhurriedly as he approached the turnstiles. As was to be expected at the end of the workday, dozens of employees were on their way out at that hour. Regan had been counting on it. He looked at the security guards who milled around at the front desk, chitchatting among themselves as people streamed out. Regan was aware that the guards had the authority to stop anybody for a search. There was a chance, however slim, that one of them would want to look into his gym bag and would rifle through the clothes and discover the classified documents concealed underneath.

But Regan was able to slide right through, unimpeded. The guards had seen him come in and go out of the building with that same gym bag hundreds of times in the past; they had no reason to suspect him. As he walked to his car, the tension draining from his body, Regan thought about how easy it had been to smuggle the documents out. He had gotten away by being just another face in the crowd, a signal drowned by a sea of noise.

In the weeks that followed, Regan removed hundreds of pages of documents from the office in his gym bag, transferring his holdings, bit by bit, into the basement of his town house in Bowie. None of the things he'd collected over the years—comic books, baseball cards, action figures—had made him rich; now, finally, he was hoarding materials with real value that he expected to convert into a fortune.

His stash wasn't limited to documents anymore. He was copying information from the NRO's computers onto CD-ROMs, which were even more convenient to smuggle out of the office. His supervisors had put him in charge of maintaining a small library of training videos on VHS tape containing instructions for accessing NRO systems. He took them home, knowing that they wouldn't be missed since he was the custodian. Late at night, while Anette and the kids slept, he would go down to the basement and copy the tapes.

It was around the same time, in April of 2000, that Regan started working on a plan to market what he had stolen. From the spy cases he had researched, he knew he would have to contact the intelligence services of the countries he was targeting. The simplest way to do so would be to walk into the embassies of these countries in the United States. But that would be dumb, Regan quickly realized, for the FBI kept a close watch on foreign embassies in the country. To minimize the risk of being found out through surveillance, he would make contact anonymously and remain incognito throughout the transaction, exchanging information for money without ever meeting with a foreign agent.

Regan began writing a letter addressed to the head of the Libyan intelligence service, whose name he had dug up on Intelink. Introducing himself as a CIA analyst, he highlighted some of the secrets he was willing to offer in exchange for $13 million. By the time he was done typing up his detailed instructions for how the transaction was to occur—the Libyans would have to set up an 800 number for him to call, and communicate that through a used-car ad in the *Washington Post*—the letter had run to thirteen pages. Drafting it was only the first step, however. To be secure, Regan decided he had to communicate the letter in code.

He had first become acquainted with codes during his training at Goodfellow shortly after he enlisted. What he'd learned about cryptology back then, going back nearly two decades, didn't go beyond the basics. But he'd been fascinated with encryption ever since. He'd even used it in his personal life. Once, after having met up with a woman behind Anette's back, he'd encrypted her name and number on a piece of paper, converting the plaintext using a simple encryption scheme he'd learned at Goodfellow. When he found the paper on his desk some months later, however, he failed to decipher the number because he couldn't recall the encryption key.

Regan encrypted the letter using a far more complex encryption scheme. He first assigned brevity codes to the different words in his text—for example, using the code "JK" to represent the word "signals." This encoded version of the letter he then converted, through further encryption, into another string of letters and numbers. In a separate document, Regan typed up the steps for decrypting the letter. After weeks of painstaking effort, he had what he thought was a foolproof way of reaching out to the Libyans without risking his anonymity.

In July, when Anette and the kids were away in Sweden, Regan went through the trove of classified materials in his basement. By now, he had more than twenty thousand pages, in addition to CD-ROMs and videotapes. He'd made multiple copies of some of the documents over the course of many visits to the high-speed copy room at his office. These were images and reports that he believed would be valued by more than one country and hence could be sold separately to each.

Sitting at home, he sorted the information by target country, bundling the printouts and CDs and tapes into packages intended for Libya and Iraq—the two that he felt most optimistic about selling to. He separated about five thousand pages of documents into another pile. They contained what Regan believed to be the most sensitive of all the secrets he had pilfered—secrets that would severely compromise the national security of the United States.

He packed these documents in Tupperware containers, along with CD-ROMs and videotapes containing information of similarly high sensitivity. He put the containers—and whatever he couldn't fit into them—into garbage bags and wrapped them up into packages, securing them with duct tape.

In the middle of a rainy day in July, Regan drove out to Patapsco Valley State Park, near Baltimore, about thirty miles from his house. The woods in the park were lush green, the hiking trails damp from rain. Regan got out of the car with a backpack and walked into the forest, his six-foot-four figure dwarfed by the surrounding trees.

After he'd trekked deep into the forest, Regan stopped and looked around. There wasn't anybody in sight. He took out a shovel from his backpack and began digging a hole in an open patch between the trees. The air was hot and humid, and by the time he'd dug a foot and a half into the ground, Regan's brow was beaded with sweat. He dropped one of the packages into the hole and covered it up with dirt.

Then he walked over to a tree several feet away and hammered some roofing nails into it. Next, he reached into his backpack and pulled out a GPS logger that he'd brought home from work. He'd used the device hundreds of times before to record the positions of air defense systems deployed in training exercises. He peered at the logger's screen to read out the coordinates of where he stood, next to the tree he'd just marked with the nails, and wrote them down on a piece of paper.

Over two more visits to the park, Regan finished burying all of the seven packages that he'd determined to be highly sensitive. On the last visit, he walked all the way to the edge of the park, without realizing that he had set foot on private property. As he was digging a hole, he heard a dog bark less than fifty yards away. He nervously finished burying the last package, hammered the nails into the nearest tree, and jotted down the location's latitude and longitude, hoping that the dog hadn't drawn anybody's attention to him. Relieved to see nobody around, he walked back to his car with his backpack and the coordinates of all seven burial sites.

He wasn't going to trade these secrets for money. Their value was much greater. They were part of his insurance plan.

CHAPTER 5

SPY HUNT

Regan pressed his foot hard on the gas pedal as he pulled out of the parking lot of TRW in the middle of the day on May 23, 2001. He'd been working at the defense contracting company's offices in Chantilly since the fall, after having retired from the Air Force in August 2000. The company planned to assign him back to the NRO as a contract employee to do the same kind of work he'd been doing before. But for now, while he waited to regain his security clearance—it had been effectively suspended upon his retirement—he didn't have a lot to keep himself busy.

Except his paranoia. Since November, when he had mailed his secret offer to the Libyans, crossing a point of no return, his mind had been gripped by an ever-present fear of being found out. It was true that he'd taken every precaution to stay anonymous. He couldn't help but think about the enormous risks he had taken by first stealing and stashing classified information, and then making contact with a hostile intelligence service, neither of which could be undone. From all the counterintelligence investigations he had read about on Intelink, he knew he was playing a dangerous game in which one wrong move could give him away. He found himself worrying constantly about being watched. He had to make sure that wasn't the case.

That's why he'd recently taken to getting on the subway and then hopping off at the last minute, right before the doors closed, to see if anybody stepped out of the train to shadow him. On this morning, just a short while after he'd come into work, he drove away from TRW and sped through the streets of Chantilly, darting glances at the rearview mirror. As he approached an exit for Interstate 66, he swerved from the left lane all the way over to the right, just in time to get on the ramp for I-66 West. If a car was following him, he assumed, it would have to switch lanes as suddenly as he had, revealing itself to him. He raced on at breakneck speed for ten miles and got off at an exit for Manassas National Battlefield Park.

Entering the park, he drove up a one-way dirt road. When he got halfway to the end, he stopped the van and turned off the engine.

He scanned his surroundings. There were no cars driving up from behind, which he took to be a reassuring sign. He sat there for twenty minutes, watching for any activity that might indicate surveillance. He saw none.

An old pickup truck drove past; it looked like nothing out of the ordinary. Regan stepped out of the van. He walked a few yards into the forested area by the road and placed a couple of *Mad* magazines on the ground. Then he hopped back into the van and returned to work, stopping for lunch along the way.

Later that day, he drove back to the park to retrieve the magazines.

They were exactly where he had left them. He felt certain he wasn't being watched.

He was wrong.

The FBI began surveilling Brian Regan in late April 2001, shortly after Steven Carr and his fellow investigators had linked the Intelink documents in the intercepted package to Regan's computer at the NRO. In the bureau, this initial monitoring of a suspect goes by the euphemism "get to know you." Teams of surveillance specialists followed him on his commute from home to TRW's offices in Chantilly and back. Regan took a bus from home to the subway, switched trains to get to a metro stop near Chantilly, and then boarded another bus to get to the parking lot of an apartment building where he kept his van. The vehicle was in such precarious condition that Regan didn't trust it enough to drive it all the way from Bowie to Chantilly, using it only for the last leg of the commute.

Surveillance is one of the most resource-intensive tasks in law enforcement. Investigative agencies like the FBI and the Drug Enforcement Administration often have to deploy dozens of people to monitor a single target. Case agents are under constant pressure to justify committing so many resources to shadowing a suspect, since there's never any guarantee that the surveillance will yield something useful. How to know if the target is the right one to focus on? How to be certain that the investigation is on the right track?

If there were any doubts in Carr's mind about Regan being the spy, they were laid to rest on May 23 when surveillance teams observed Regan driving like a lunatic from TRW to Manassas Battlefield National Park. Just because Regan had failed to notice any cars following him didn't mean there weren't any. When Regan was parked on the dirt road, Carr was on the phone with a surveillance specialist nicknamed Smitty, who was watching Regan's van from a distance.

"We've got a live one," Smitty told Carr.

"What do you mean?" Carr asked.

Smitty described how Regan had been driving and how he'd come to a stop in the middle of nowhere.

"What are you doing?" Carr wanted to know.

Smitty said surveillance couldn't possibly drive up the dirt road in the car they were using. It would look suspicious.

"Do you have any pickup trucks or anything?"

"Yes, we do," Smitty answered. Soon after, the team had a pickup truck drive by Regan's van. Smitty called Carr back.

"He's just sitting in the van."

None of these observations constituted evidence that would help Carr build his case. They wouldn't have any value in court. Regan hadn't broken any laws by leaving a couple of magazines in the park and collecting them later. But his unusual behavior showed that he was watching to see if he was being watched. In Carr's eyes, it was undeniable proof of guilt.

After the five-hour flight from Washington, D.C., to San Diego, Regan could have used a shower and a nap to get over his jet lag. Instead, he picked up a rental car at the airport and headed south, toward Mexico.

After driving for two hours, he parked the car next to a highway on the U.S. side of the border with Mexico. He'd brought along a voice-activated recorder that he placed on top of one of the rear tires. From where he'd parked, he rode a shuttle bus that took him across the border into Mexico, where he wandered about in a shopping mall.

Returning to the car a couple of hours later, he retrieved the recorder and played it back. If anybody had approached the vehicle in his absence, he expected the recorder to turn on.

There was just one complication, however—one key detail that Regan hadn't thought of. The noise of traffic from the highway, it turned out, was enough to activate the recorder. When Regan listened to it, all he could hear was the sound of vehicles roaring past.

He played the audio again and again, trying to listen for evidence that his security had been compromised. He was finally convinced that it hadn't.

Satisfied, he boarded a flight back to Washington, D.C. The trip's only purpose had been to check for surveillance. He was exhausted from traveling from the East Coast to the West Coast and back in the span of a day, but no effort was too much for him in his quest for operational security.

And in that, he had succeeded. For when he got off the plane at Reagan National Airport in D.C. to execute the next step in his plan, the FBI's surveillance teams still had no idea where he was.

It was evening when Regan left the airport, driving a rental SUV. He had another trip to make, but first he needed to make a stop at home in Bowie. He had to pack a few things.

He had written them down on a checklist. One was a GPS navigator—a Garmin III—that he'd recently bought for $320. He wouldn't have had to purchase it if he'd been able to keep the GPS device given to him at the NRO, but he'd had to turn that in when he retired. He'd also ordered a pair of night-vision goggles ten days before flying to San Diego; when he got to the house, he was glad to find that they had arrived. At $245, the goggles were a pricey purchase, but he was sure he was going to need them.

He put them in his backpack, along with the GPS. There were sundry other items on his list, and he crossed them out one by one.

> Shovel, tape measure, gloves. *Check.*
> Toothbrush, paste, razor. *Check.*
> Snacks, drinks, vodka bottle. *Check.*

When he had finished packing, Regan drove 150 miles south, past Richmond, to Chester, Virginia. His first stop was a public storage facility where he'd been renting space since the end of 2000. In there, under lock and key, were fifteen thousand pages of secret documents and other classified materials—everything he'd stolen, save what he'd buried in Patapsco Valley State Park. He'd kept the stash hidden in the basement of his house for several months before deciding that it was too risky.

He hauled the documents out of the storage unit and loaded them into the SUV. From there he drove to a nearby motel and checked into a room. With its grimy carpeting and a bed that seemed flea-ridden, the accommodations were anything but inviting. But Regan didn't care. If his plan worked, he'd never need to stay in a room like this again in his life.

He had sorted the documents before. Sitting in the room, he sorted them again, with the intention of bundling different stacks of papers into individual packages. As he thumbed through the documents, he came across a number of reports and images whose importance he hadn't quite grasped earlier.

These materials, he realized, were even more sensitive than what he'd buried in Patapsco. The secrets they contained were simply too damaging to be sold.

He set them aside.

It was the oddest of all the choices he had made since the summer of 1999 when he began contemplating espionage. He had rationalized the idea of betraying the country for money because he'd convinced himself that the U.S. government hadn't treated him fairly. He'd spelled out that self-justification in his offer to the Libyans. If basketball players and Hollywood stars in the United States could make millions, he had written, surely he deserved more than just a pension for the years of service to his country.

That rationale had driven him onward in his conspiracy, and he had marched forward, steadily, unhesitatingly, until this moment, when he found himself staring at a line he didn't want to cross. For somebody who had spent months masterminding a traitorous scheme, it was strange to be acting out of any sense of loyalty toward the country. But even treason has its limits, and Regan had reached as far as he was willing to go. He couldn't let this subset of documents fall into anybody's hands.

He didn't want to risk holding on to them, either. There was no question of bringing them back to the NRO. The only option he had was to destroy them.

He went into the bathroom and turned on the bathtub faucet. When the tub filled up with a couple of inches of water, he put the sheaf of documents in it, letting the pages soak. He watched as the water turned cloudy from the ink dissolving off the documents. Mangling the wet papers with his hands, he turned them into a soggy, mulchlike mess.

He picked up the dripping mass from the tub and tried flushing it down the toilet, realizing immediately what a terrible idea that was. The toilet got clogged and overflowed. Before things could get worse, he fished the pulp out of the water and put it into a garbage bag. Stepping out of the motel into a nearby alley, he tossed the bag into a dumpster and walked away.

Returning to his room, Regan stuffed the remaining pages into Tupperware containers and cardboard boxes and wrapped them up in garbage bags. When he was done, he had before him twelve packages in all. They sat on the mattress and the floor, looking like nondescript goods at a warehouse. To Regan, they might as well have been gold bricks.

Taking six of the packages with him, he drove to Pocahontas State Park, twenty miles away. As he entered the park, the noise of traffic faded away. He left the vehicle at a parking lot and followed a hiking trail into the woods, the sound of his footsteps accentuated by the stillness of the night. He had put on the night-vision goggles to begin with, but they were bulky and soon proved to be a bother. There was enough light for him to be able to see clearly without them. He took them off and trekked on through the trees. He was far away from the park's camping grounds and picnic tables. The handle of a shovel, which he'd shortened with a saw, poked out of the top of his backpack like an antenna.

After walking for several minutes, he veered off the trail and stopped at a clearing. He lowered the backpack, pulled out the shovel, and began digging, carefully piling the dirt on a plastic sheet to avoid leaving any sign of the dig. When the hole was big enough, he dropped a package in and covered it up, packing up the leftover dirt in the plastic sheet. Then, as he'd done in Patapsco, he hammered nails into a nearby tree and measured the distance from it to the burial site with his tape measure. From the Garmin, he jotted down the latitude and longitude of the location.

Regan buried the remaining five packages in similar fashion that night. Then he drove back to the motel, completely exhausted. He would return to the park the following night to bury the other set of six packages.

On the evening of June 13, investigative specialist Ronald Good sat at a desk inside the Crofton Community Library in Maryland, flipping through a magazine. His colleague William Wickman stood a few feet away, scanning the titles on the shelves. To a casual observer, it would have seemed like the two men were absorbed in their own worlds. But in fact, their attention was focused on Brian Regan.

Regan had resurfaced only days before, in early June, following a vanishing act that had lasted for the better part of a week. Ever since, the bureau's surveillance personnel had intensified their watch on him, hoping not to lose him again. On this evening, Good and Wickman and other members of their team had followed Regan from TRW's offices to the Crofton library. A little past seven p.m., after Regan entered the library and sat down at one of the computers, Good walked over and seated himself behind him. Wickman, who was watching from farther away, took out a camera and snapped a photo of Regan from behind a bookcase.

They could tell that Regan had an Internet browser open on the screen, but it was hard to see what he was looking at. After half an hour of surfing, Regan got up, collected some printouts, and left.

Good rose from his chair, eager to get to the computer Regan had been using. Before he could reach it, however, a woman took the spot. He bided his time while the woman searched the library's catalog for the next several minutes.

When she got up, he grabbed the seat. Wickman came over to join him. They noticed that Regan had forgotten to close the Internet browser. He'd merely minimized the window before he left the terminal.

With a click of the mouse, Wickman maximized it. Hitting the "back" button over and over, he was able to retrieve many of the pages that Regan had looked at throughout his surfing session. The surveillance specialists couldn't believe their luck. After going to incredible lengths to detect surveillance, Regan had failed to do the simplest of things to cover his tracks. If he'd taken the trouble to exit the browser, tracing his surfing activity on the terminal would have been a much harder task. Since it was a public computer, the browser wasn't set up to store any history once users ended their sessions.

Wickman clicked through the pages, printing them out as he went. Regan had spent time on the Lycos search engine, entering terms like "Embassies of the Arab world," "Libyan embassy," "consulate of Libya." In the pages showing the results, certain Web links were highlighted in purple—these were the sites that Regan had clicked on. From the searches and the highlighted links, it was evident that Regan had looked for the addresses of Libyan embassies and consulates in a number of foreign countries, including France and Switzerland. He had also looked up Iraqi embassies.

What Wickman and his colleagues gleaned that evening wasn't enough for Carr to figure out Regan's next move. But it gave the FBI more evidence to press for authority under the Foreign Intelligence Surveillance Act (FISA) to listen to Regan's telephone calls and to ask for resources to watch him around the clock instead of sixteen hours a day. Carr had submitted the FISA request eight weeks earlier, supporting it with all the evidence that pointed to Regan as the sender of the letters. But reviewers in the Office of Intelligence Policy and Review at the Department of Justice—the unit responsible for obtaining the required permission from FISA court—still doubted that the FBI had done enough to exclude all other potential suspects.

There were good reasons for the DOJ to be cautious. The FBI had made a grave mistake in a recent high-profile counterespionage investigation. Agents had spent years investigating a CIA officer named Brian Kelly on the suspicion that he was a KGB mole. Their determined pursuit of Kelly as the prime suspect in the case all but broke the man. He was followed 24/7; his phone was tapped; his family members were subjected to interrogation. He was suspended from the CIA for a year without pay. It was only in late 2000 that the FBI found evidence showing that the mole agents had been looking for was in fact not Kelly but one of the bureau's own: Russian counterintelligence analyst Robert Hanssen. Even though the FBI was subsequently able to redeem itself by arresting Hanssen in February 2001, the episode had made some in the DOJ wary of future mistakes.

The surveillance at the Crofton library gave Carr the ammunition to remove any doubts that the OIPR had. It was too much of a coincidence for Regan to be searching for addresses of Libyan and Iraqi embassies—using the anonymity afforded by a public library—unless he was the sender of the offer the FBI had intercepted.

The FISA authority was granted within forty-eight hours, and agents promptly began eavesdropping on Regan's phone calls. Most were short conversations between him and Anette about household matters. Regan was clearly the less talkative of the two, rarely responding to Anette in more than monosyllables. It didn't seem that anything useful could be gleaned from tapping his phones. Then, in one call, agents heard Regan mention upcoming travel, although it wasn't clear where he would be traveling.

The answer emerged over the next few days. On June 20, as surveillance specialists watched Regan riding the subway, they saw him looking at a foldout map. He tore out a section of it, and at his stop (or similar), he got off the train, leaving the rest of the map tucked in the gap between his seat and the side of the compartment. James Bond would have been appalled.

Despite his abundance of caution, Regan wasn't immune to this kind of complacence. In fact, his absentmindedness, investigators would come to realize, made him prone to it.

The surveillance team collected the foldout. It was a map of Switzerland. The section Regan had taken with him was the part that covered the city of Bern. Four days later, Regan was once again seen at the Crofton library, this time researching youth hostels in Bern and Zurich in addition to embassy addresses in France, Switzerland, and Germany. Checking with various airlines, investigators learned that Regan was set to fly to Berlin on June 26 and return to the United States on July 3.

For U.S. law enforcement to conduct surveillance in another country is tricky business, for it could mean violating the laws of that country. That's not to say the FBI never does it. But in Regan's case, there was simply not enough time for agents to come up with a plan to watch him in Europe. Carr was worried that his quarry was going dark again, but there was nothing he could do about it. All he could hope was that Regan would come back.

As Lufthansa Flight 415 took off from Washington's Dulles International Airport for Berlin, Regan gazed out of the window and thought about the mission that lay ahead. He had accomplished what he had always believed to be the hardest part of his plan: accumulating a trove of secrets and stashing them. He had assumed that selling the information would be a cakewalk in comparison. But that expectation hadn't panned out. For more than two months after having written to Libyan intelligence in November 2000, he had diligently scanned the classified section of the *Washington Post*, expecting to spot the used-car ad he'd asked them to place to initiate contact. He'd seen nothing of the sort. Frustrated, he'd stopped looking.

However, he wasn't willing to give up on the plan after having come so far. There was simply too much riding on it. In the months since he'd begun stealing documents, the mountain of debt he faced had only grown bigger. He had even had to forge Anette's signature to apply for new credit cards. Meanwhile, Anette had purchased for $6,000 a horse that she was having shipped from Sweden later that summer. Anybody with an inkling of the couple's financial situation would have called her crazy, but Regan hadn't raised objections. Given the millions of dollars he was expecting from his espionage, $6,000 seemed like pocket change.

He had thought long and hard about why the Libyans hadn't responded. Perhaps his offer hadn't reached the right person within Libyan intelligence. Perhaps they had been wary of dealing with somebody who was hell-bent on remaining anonymous. The thing to do, he had concluded, was to relax his condition of anonymity. He would make contact with potential buyers face-to-face. He'd have to go knocking on doors like a salesman.

It would have been convenient for Regan to walk into the Libyan embassy in Washington, D.C. But he had learned enough about American counterintelligence to know how closely the FBI monitored foreign embassies and consulates in the United States. There was no way he would be able to get in undetected. That's why he'd decided to fly to Europe, where he was certain of being able to try his luck without risk.

Having landed in Berlin, Regan traveled to Munich and then on to Bern. He'd brought along a map of the city, which serves as Switzerland's de facto capital. (The country has no officially declared capital city.) The address he was looking for was Tavelweg 2, CH 3006. It was just east of downtown, a mile from the scenic Aare River, which winds through Bern.

He had no trouble getting to it. An elegant two-story mansion stood there, in the middle of a lush green lawn fenced in from the sidewalk by a row of hedges. The flags of Libya and Switzerland fluttered inside the compound. On the wall next to an iron gate leading into the property was a plate that read: EMBASSY OF THE GREAT SOCIALIST PEOPLE'S LIBYAN ARAB JAMAHIRIYA. It was the official name that President Muammar Gaddhafi had given to the country in 1977, a few years after coming to power through a military coup.

Regan walked in. Going up to the front desk, he asked to speak to the security officer. He didn't offer an introduction, although it was obvious from his accent that he was American.

A while later, a member of the staff led him into a back room. Regan explained that he had access to secret information that could be of value to the Libyan government. He could only discuss his offer with a senior official, he said, somebody who had the authority to handle intelligence matters.

The staffer, who wasn't fluent in English, indicated that he was having trouble understanding Regan. He had Regan sit at a computer and asked him to type up his request so that it could be passed on to the right officials.

Regan had thought he would be welcomed with open arms. And here he was having to struggle with a language barrier just to get to the negotiating table. Was this really how a spy with reams of secrets in his possession deserved to be treated? It was maddening.

Regan sat at the computer and began typing a message, expecting it to be a last formality before he got his desired meeting. But while he was in the middle of it, an official walked in demanding to know how the embassy staff had allowed an unknown American to come in.

Regan didn't get a chance to explain. He was marched out of the building. "Don't ever come back," the official told him.

Regan couldn't understand why he had been kicked out. He had no idea that walk-ins, or volunteer spies, were treated suspiciously by intelligence services around the world. To the embassy authorities, Regan had in all likelihood come across as a dangle— an agent sent to gain their trust and gather intelligence on behalf of an enemy. He might have had a better chance of establishing his credibility if he'd first identified the right security official— perhaps by watching the embassy gates for employees who arrived at work in expensive cars—and then approaching that official at a different venue, like a parking lot.

Troubled as he was by the failure, Regan didn't see it as the end of the road. He made the most of the rest of his stay in Europe, binge-drinking and sightseeing in Nice and Zurich. He made a phone call to Anette to tell her that he'd been out in the field working. Then he flew back to Washington, no less determined to succeed.

With Regan back in the United States, the FBI pondered its next move. The bureau still didn't have enough evidence to arrest Regan. To question him at this stage could ruin the prospects of ever finding out precisely what he had done. At the same time, Carr realized that simply waiting and watching wasn't enough. The FBI had to make every effort to catch Regan red-handed in the act of espionage.

Regan's new employer—TRW—knew nothing about the investigation. The company was waiting for him to get back his security clearance so that he could do the work he'd been hired for. Since Regan had a foreign-born spouse, the process was expected to take longer than usual, because of some additional security reviews. Still, more than ten months had passed since TRW had submitted the application for his clearance to the Department of Defense, and company managers were beginning to get impatient. In February, Regan's supervisor at TRW had written a letter to the Pentagon urging authorities to accelerate the approval process. But in May, the company had been told that Regan's paperwork needed to be resubmitted, which meant the clearance could take another few months.

On July 24, Carr went to the NRO. He brought along his laptop, on which he'd prepared a PowerPoint presentation about the case. The audience for his briefing was the senior leadership of the NRO. They had gathered in the conference room of the NRO director, Keith Hall.

With his round, mustachioed countenance and smiling demeanor, Hall could have been easily cast as a jolly uncle in a Christmas movie. His genial air belied an independent mindedness that had served him well over the years. Hall had begun his intelligence career in the Army, commanding two field intelligence units during the 1970s. He had gone on to serve for eight years as a staff member on the Senate Select Committee on Intelligence before moving to the Pentagon in 1991 as the deputy assistant secretary of defense for intelligence and security. Hall had been appointed director of the NRO in 1997, at a time when the agency was facing heat from Congress for financial mismanagement that had led to the disappearance of $4 billion in funds. Even by the standards of fraud and wastage in defense spending, it was not an inconsiderable amount of money to have gone missing, and so, since taking over, Hall had focused most of his attention on improving the accountability of how the NRO spent its vast budget.

A different kind of accountability was on his mind as he sat down for the briefing. Hall had learned about Regan from his staff in the spring and had lost a lot of sleep in the months since, worrying about the extent of the damage that might have been caused. As with finances, the buck on security, too, stopped with the director's office.

He sat at one end of a long conference table. Carr sat at the other end, in front of a briefing board. There were more than a dozen other people in the room, including Debra Donahoo, the head of counterintelligence at the NRO. The mood was somber as Carr went through his slides over the next forty-five minutes, providing a detailed timeline of the investigation and where things stood. Then, looking straight at Hall, he laid out a couple of options.

One was to grant Regan his security clearance and have him come back to the NRO. "You can put him back into a position of access," Carr said. "We will surveil him. We will apply every FISA technique we can possibly apply. We will watch his every move and we'll guard your equities to the best of our abilities."

The other option was to deny Regan the clearance. "You say

no, he goes back out on the street. He tries to find a security job someplace else," Carr told the group. In that event, the FBI would just have to pursue Regan wherever he went next. The NRO would no longer be involved in the investigation.

However, there was a downside to shutting Regan out of the NRO, Carr pointed out. It would make it hard for the FBI to find out what classified information Regan had taken and what he'd done with it. "We may never find out where that information is," Carr said.

It couldn't have been clearer which of the two options Carr was recommending.

Hall looked around the table at his deputies. None of them was keen to endorse Carr's proposal. Some were strongly opposed. It was bad enough for the NRO that a spy had been able to operate within the organization for months without raising any red flags. To knowingly let him come back and possibly steal more information seemed like lunacy. Moreover, it was the FBI's job to hunt Regan down and uncover his whole plot. The smart thing for the NRO to do, most of Hall's deputies felt, was to limit any further liability.

Hall could see their point. The NRO would definitely be putting itself at risk by allowing Regan to have access again. If things went wrong, the NRO leadership would be held accountable for having handed an espionage suspect the keys to the kingdom. Hall would personally never be able to live down the ignominy.

Yet, he also understood—perhaps better than many in the room—the risks of failing to bring Regan to justice. Hall had become intimately familiar with the impact of espionage on national security beginning in 1985, when the FBI and its partner agencies made a string of high-profile spy arrests, including John Walker Jr. and Jonathan Pollard. The year would later come to be known as the Year of the Spy. Hall's position at the time as a staffer on the Senate Intelligence Committee had given him an appreciation of how important it was to hunt down moles and prosecute them. Years later, at the Pentagon, he had helped coordinate the government's response to the fallout from the betrayal of the CIA's Aldrich Ames, serving as the first chair of the National Counterintelligence Policy Board.

He asked Carr how the FBI planned to monitor Regan at the NRO if he was allowed to come back.

A surveillance camera would watch his work space, and every keystroke on his computer would be logged, Carr replied.

Hall looked around the table once again. Then he leaned back in his chair and clasped his hands behind his head. "We're going to do it," he said. "We're going to put him back into access." Then he brought his hands to the table and leaned forward, looking at Carr. "You have one hundred twenty days to figure this out."

CHAPTER 6

NABBED

On Monday, July 30, after a relaxing weekend trip to Virginia Beach with Anette and the kids, Regan showed up for work at his new office in an NRO building two miles from the agency's headquarters. He had received a phone call from a security officer at TRW the week before, delivering the good news he'd been waiting for since late 2000. At long last, his clearance had come through. He could finally stop worrying about his future with TRW. Not that he'd have to bother about employment for too long.

He badged in and spent the morning getting a customary security briefing. In the afternoon, an office manager led Regan to a suite he was to share with another worker. It had two workstations facing each other. Regan looked around, studying the space.

"I don't want to sit here," he said.

His eyes were on a one-person suite across the hall. It was vacant. He walked over to it and put his bag down, saying he'd prefer to sit at that desk instead of the one he'd been given. There, he would be by himself, without a coworker directly across from him.

The manager didn't see any reason to object.

But Regan's seemingly innocuous seating preference caused a stir at the NRO headquarters, where an FBI agent—along with counterintelligence officials from the NRO and the Air Force Office of Special Investigations—sat inside a conference room watching a video monitor. The agent made a phone call to Steve Carr.

"Hello," Carr answered. He'd been eagerly waiting since morning for an update.

"He's not sitting at his desk," the agent informed Carr, referring to Regan.

In the days prior—right after the NRO director gave permission to bring Regan back—investigators had worked speedily to bug the office space Regan was going to be stationed at. Carr didn't want to waste any time in putting Regan into a position of access, especially after Regan's worrying weeklong trip to Europe, which had heightened the FBI's sense of urgency. Working together, specialists from AFOSI and the FBI had installed a pinhole video camera in the ceiling right above what was to be Regan's desk.

Thanks to technological advances since the end of the Cold War, the control unit in the back end of the camera was the size of a credit card, and the tech specialists had easily been able to conceal it in the ceiling plaster. The unit was connected to a device intended to convert the camera's analogue feed into a digital signal, which could be transmitted over the NRO's network to the monitoring room at headquarters. Investigators had also installed surveillance software on the computer at the workstation, so that any activity on it could be seen in real time by agents on watch.

At the moment, however, all that the FBI agent in the monitoring room could see on the video was a vacant desk and chair. As Carr had learned time and again, no matter how well thought out an investigative plan might be, the real world has a way of throwing up last-minute surprises. It seemed impractical to install a new camera over the desk that Regan had claimed. The NRO would have to ensure that Regan sat where he was supposed to.

Making that happen was a delicate matter. As is true of any ongoing espionage investigation, the Regan case had been kept strictly confidential. Even within the FBI, the NRO, and the Air Force, only those with an absolute need to know were aware of the fact that Regan was a suspected spy. If Regan was to be placed in the monitored office space without making him suspicious, his supervisor at TRW would have to be taken into confidence.

That person was Paul McNulty, a tall, broad-shouldered former Navy captain who had hired Regan. Bob Rice, an NRO counterintelligence official, called McNulty into his office. After having McNulty sign a confidentiality agreement, Rice told him that Regan was under investigation. He didn't give McNulty any details but explained why Regan had to sit where he was supposed to.

After the briefing, McNulty went over to Regan, who was settling in.

"Brian, you have to sit over there," he said, explaining that the single-person suite had to be reserved for another employee who was expected to start in two weeks.

Reluctantly, Regan gathered up his things and moved to the other office. An aerial view of him appeared on the video monitor in the NRO conference room. The next morning, he signed on to his computer after receiving his log-in information from the IT department. Within minutes, he was on Intelink, looking at images of Libyan weapons-testing facilities in the Sahara Desert. It was as if he had never left.

In his first two weeks, Regan went through a round of training to brush up on his knowledge of satellites and other national systems used in reconnaissance. He could do it all at his desk by taking a series of core competency courses accessible on the NRO network. From sources of electronic intelligence to ways of resolving data problems, the subjects of most of the courses were familiar to him, and he was able to breeze through them. He had no difficulty either with the tests he had to take on a variety of topics—orbital mechanics, imagery intelligence, collection management, and so on— and ended up with scores of 90 to 100 percent on most.

The quick work Regan made of the courses left him with plenty of time on hand to resume his explorations on Intelink. As they monitored his browsing from their perch at the NRO—in real time rather than several months after the fact—the investigators saw that his searches were no longer confined to the Middle East and North Africa. He had added a new country to his list: the People's Republic of China.

The documents he was looking up contained secrets about the Chinese military that the United States had gathered over decades. On his third day at work, shortly before leaving the office, he spent time studying a defense intelligence assessment of sites in China holding weapons of mass destruction. He looked up an image of one of these storage facilities. Days later, he accessed a report on China's deployed ballistic missile force, and not long after, another one titled "China, Nuclear Weapons and Special Nuclear Material Security Handbook."

Even though he had no justifiable work reason to surf Intelink, Regan didn't seem to feel any trepidation in doing it, despite being new on the job. He made no effort to guard his computer screen from the eyes of coworkers. But he was still concerned about surveillance. At one point, when his coworker was absent from the room, he closed the door and got up on his desk to quickly inspect the ceiling. Fortunately for the investigators, the camera had been hidden well enough that he detected no sign of it. He went back to surfing, assured that he was in the clear.

On the morning of August 15, Regan called up two Intelink documents on his desktop. The first was an aerial image of a Chinese surface-to-surface missile launch facility. The second was an aerial image of a surface-to-air missile launcher in the northern no-fly zone of Iraq. For the next twenty minutes, agents observed him scribbling on a five-by-seven yellow legal pad while glancing repeatedly at the screen. He appeared to be making notes.

It was the first time that agents had seen him engage in this behavior. Their eyes glued to the video monitor, they awaited his next move. Regan closed the documents that were open on the screen, took out a three-by-five index card, and began writing on it, this time consulting the notes he'd made on the pad. Then he took a pair of scissors and cut out the bottom of the index card before slipping it into his front pocket. Next, he ripped the top few sheets from the pad, tore them up into little pieces, and threw them into a burn bag—a trash receptacle for discarding classified information.

Around five p.m. that day, agents watched Regan take out the scissors again. This time, he used them to cut out parts of documents that contained text printed on a dark background. It was impossible for the monitoring agents to discern from the video monitor what these documents were. Regan took the pieces he'd cut out and taped them together on a plain sheet, which he then put into a folder. He balled up what remained of the documents and threw that into the burn bag.

Late at night on August 16, long after all employees had left the building, Carr and others went in to do a search of Regan's office. In the burn bag, they found the crumpled-up remains of the dark-colored documents that Regan had cut out portions of. The pages were from a course catalog containing descriptions of secret and top secret courses available to employees of the NRO and other intelligence agencies. Reading the catalog could provide a foreign intelligence service useful insight into NRO systems.

The investigators also recovered the torn-up bits of paper from the pad that Regan had been writing on. He had not ripped out just the top sheet that contained his notes but several sheets below it as well, apparently to ensure he didn't leave behind any indentations of his writing.

Carr pieced the puzzle together. At the top of the page, Regan had written "August 7, 2001," followed by a series of digits and letters: "IRBMCSS2." The information tallied with the Chinese missile launch facility whose image Regan had looked at: the digits were the latitude and longitude, August 7 was the date the image was taken, and IRBMCSS2 stood for the type of weapon system it was—intermediate-range ballistic missile Chinese surface-to-surface 2. On the next line, Regan had jotted down the image date and coordinates for the Iraqi surface-to-air missile launcher whose surveillance photograph he'd browsed along with the Chinese facility.

What Regan had scribbled farther down was more intriguing. He'd written each of the coordinates across two lines in zigzag fashion, like two sets of sawteeth interlocked with each other. The first digit of the Chinese coordinates was penned on the top line, the second digit on the line below, the third digit again on the top line, and so on. The digits of the Iraqi coordinates were similarly arranged, starting on the lower line and alternating up and down. From the resulting pattern, Regan had derived a single sequence of digits that consisted of the two sets of coordinates intermingled with each other, which he'd written on another part of the sheet and scratched out because he'd made an error. The jottings, as Carr soon learned, were steps to encipher the two sets of coordinates using a simple technique known as a rail-fence cipher. Regan had also written a series of words at the bottom of the sheet—"could sit should" and "stand and mingle." It didn't take long for Carr to recognize that they were an innocuous code for the two weapons systems in the aerial images: CSS and SAM.

Days before the FBI agents watched him take notes at his desk, Regan e-mailed his supervisor—Paul McNulty—to say he would be taking some time off at the end of August. The request was an unusual one to make for an employee who had just started in a new job—that, too, after waiting in the wings for the better part of a year—but Regan explained that he had to take his wife and kids to Orlando for vacation before the school year started. McNulty didn't object, and Regan put down the dates he would be gone on an office whiteboard where employees posted their whereabouts. Next to his name on the employee list, he scrawled, with a fat blue marker: "27–30 August, Leave, Orlando, FL."

In fact, he was getting ready for another trip to Europe to market himself as a spy. Using his frequent-flier miles on United Airlines, he had purchased a return ticket from Washington Dulles to Frankfurt—flying out on August 23 and coming back on August

30—for a mere $31.26. According to the terms of his security clearance, he was supposed to inform the NRO of any foreign travel in advance. Following that rule, he had decided, wouldn't be a smart thing for him to do. It could lead to some uncomfortable questions about the purpose of his travel.

On the weekend before he was to fly out of the country, Regan drove to Farmingdale with Anette and the kids. He had finally had to cave in and buy another minivan to replace the old Dodge, which hadn't stopped breaking down even after he spent $5,000 to put in a new engine. He was convinced that the repair shop had taken him for a ride. He had sent angry letters to the shop, threatening to go to court, but to no avail.

But bygones were bygones. The best he could do now was focus on the future. A lot was riding on it. His $65,000 salary from TRW was considerably higher than what he'd been making as a master sergeant, but it wasn't enough to keep pace with the family's needs, let alone get out of debt. Both his daughters needed braces, and that wasn't going to be cheap. The older daughter was about to start high school, which worried Regan. He had heard about incidents of kids bringing weapons to the high school she would be going to beginning the next month, and he wished to move to a better neighborhood. He would be able to afford that and more if he succeeded in making a sale this time when he traveled to Europe.

Before that, he wanted to squeeze in a visit to see his parents. It was the last chance to take his kids to the beach before the summer ended. One of his brothers was hosting a block party that weekend, which he was looking forward to. But that wasn't all.

He also had some business to take care of.

On the morning of Saturday, August 18, Regan left Anette and the kids with his parents and drove to Farmingdale High School. He parked his car and walked into the woods behind the handball courts and spent about fifteen minutes there before driving back to his parents' house. The next morning, he drove out by himself once again and went to Staples to make copies of documents he'd brought along. From there, he drove a couple of miles to Highway 110, parking on the grassy shoulder in front of an exit sign for Huntington and Amityville.

He stepped out of the car and once again disappeared into a wooded area nearby. From the other side of the highway, a surveillance specialist shot video of him entering the woods and then coming out ten minutes later. But just like at Farmingdale High the day before, even with a powerful telephoto lens, it was impossible to peer into the middle of the trees and see what he'd been up to. Following him all the way in would have given the surveillance away.

And so it was that by Sunday night, as Regan drove back to Bowie with his family, investigators realized that despite having learned a great deal about how he had spent his weekend—from where he and the family had gone out to eat (Mario's Pizza) to what movie he'd watched at the movie theater with Anette and his boys (*Jurassic Park III*)—they were in the dark about what really mattered. What had Regan made copies of at Staples and why had he gone into the woods two mornings in a row?

At around eight twenty-five a.m. on August 23, Paul McNulty stopped by Regan's desk to have Regan accompany him to a meeting at NRO headquarters. It was Regan's last working day before his leave—although he'd written August 27 to 30 on the office whiteboard, he planned to take Friday, August 24, off as well. As the two chitchatted on the short drive to the NRO in McNulty's car, Regan told McNulty that he would be getting on the road after work to head to Orlando with his family.

The meeting was in the Signals Applications Office, where Regan had worked until 2000. Some of his former coworkers were present. Regan, dressed in a polo shirt with broad stripes, sat down with McNulty to participate in the discussion, which was focused on a proposal to make changes to the system for disseminating the NRO's satellite intelligence to other branches of the military.

Regan listened to the presentation with his typically aloof expression. When the speaker had laid out the proposal, McNulty turned to him to ask what he thought.

"Do you know anything about this?" McNulty asked.

"Yeah," Regan said, getting up from his chair to walk up to the whiteboard.

He sketched out a flowchart showing how the NRO's intelligence was pushed out to different military customers. There was no need to change the system, he explained, because the intelligence was already accessible to all the users it was meant for. By the end of the meeting, most people in the room appeared convinced by his argument.

"It's a good thing I took you to that meeting," McNulty remarked as he and Regan drove back to their building. "I didn't know anything about that system."

In McNulty's estimate, the proposed changes could have cost a few million dollars. "You just saved the government a bunch of money," he said admiringly.

Although McNulty's compliment was perfectly sincere, bringing Regan to the meeting had been nothing but a ruse. McNulty was acting at the direction of NRO counterintelligence, which had asked him to keep Regan away from his office for a block of time that morning.

Investigators had found out about Regan's plans to travel to Europe less than twenty-four hours earlier. Although they had previously guessed that Regan might be lying about going to Orlando—they hadn't heard him mention it even once in phone conversations with his wife—his itinerary had come to light only at the last minute after an agent made inquiries with various airlines and discovered reservations under Regan's name on Lufthansa. His flight was to take off from Dulles at four-oh-five p.m.

When Carr and his colleagues came into work that morning, the atmosphere at the FBI's Washington Field Office was crackling with tension. Everybody could sense that a big day lay ahead. But whether Regan was to be arrested or not was still an open question that had to be resolved by senior officials in the Department of Justice. The FBI could put Regan in handcuffs only after getting the DOJ's authorization.

It wasn't clear if the evidence Carr and his fellow investigators had collected up to this point was enough to convict Regan. What they had been hoping all along was to catch him in the act of providing classified information to a foreign intelligence service. At the very least, they wanted direct evidence showing that he had contacted another government with the intention of transmitting U.S. defense secrets.

Using the intercepted packages to prove that wasn't an option, for that would involve revealing how the FBI got the packages in the first place. To establish the provenance of the packages, the government would be compelled to call the confidential informant who had provided the packages to testify in court. Not only would that put the informant at risk; it would deter other sources from tipping off the bureau in the future. The cost to the FBI's broader counterintelligence efforts would be much too high.

The investigators were anxious to find some new evidence that would provide unambiguous grounds for an arrest. But the clock was ticking toward his scheduled departure. With Regan away at the meeting with McNulty, Carr and his fellow agents made another sweep of his office. In the video surveillance from the prior weeks, they had seen Regan occasionally bringing a personal laptop to work, and Carr was optimistic about finding something incriminating on it. The investigators searched every corner of his work space, even crawling under his desk, but there was no laptop to be examined.

Outside, in the building's parking lot, another group of agents searched Regan's van. In a blue duffel bag that looked like a carry-on he was planning to take on the flight, they found a blue folder containing Regan's airline tickets, a Eurail pass for train travel within Europe, European railway maps, four blank envelopes, and several blank mailing labels. Also tucked in the folder were papers that looked decidedly more curious.

The pages were filled with line after line of three-digit numbers written by hand. They consisted of three copies of a set of three documents, each titled "Letter." Two of them—Letter S-I134 and Letter M-I134—consisted of a single page each, while the third, marked Letter A-341I, ran to two pages. The multiple lines of trinomials in the documents looked like possible code. It was impossible to say whether these "letters" were the evidence investigators were looking for.

The agents photographed the sheets and the other items in the folder, hoping that nobody was watching. Then they carefully put everything back in the duffel bag as before, locked the van, and cleared out of the lot as quickly as possible.

At twelve fifteen p.m., in another parking lot ten miles away—right next to Dulles Airport—Special Agent Bill Lace stepped out of his car to brief a team of FBI personnel. He had rounded up more than two dozen agents and staff from the Washington Field Office to put together a plan for searching Regan's luggage at the airport that afternoon. Although the duffel bag had already been searched, investigators didn't know what else Regan was planning to take along on the trip, and they wanted to be prepared to look through all of his belongings—including checked baggage and other carry-ons—before he got to the departure gate.

For the briefing, Lace had asked everybody to meet in the parking lot of the Courtyard Marriott near Dulles. As they were gathering, one of the FBI's surveillance specialists drove up to Lace to deliver an urgent message.

"Cast Led is here!" he yelled from inside the car, using the bureau's code name for Regan.

"What are you talking about?" Lace asked, surprised.

"He's right on the other side of the parking lot!"

The surveillance team had seen Regan leave his office building an hour and a half earlier, soon after he and McNulty returned from the NRO. He'd first driven to a Staples, and then to the

Courtyard Marriott, arriving there exactly at the same time that Lace and his colleagues were assembling there.

"OK, everybody back to their car!" Lace told the others, hurriedly reentering his own parked vehicle. If Regan were to notice the huddle in the middle of the lot, he would definitely have reason to be suspicious, and that could seriously jeopardize the investigation.

The group scattered. Sitting in his car, Lace scanned the other end of the parking lot. He finally spotted Regan's van, from which he saw Regan emerge and walk into the hotel through a side entrance. Minutes later, much to Lace's relief, he returned to the van and drove away.

From the hotel, Regan drove to the airport. His flight wasn't until a few hours later, but he wanted to check in early. The Lufthansa counter hadn't opened yet, however, and he had to wait for an hour before he was able to drop off his suitcase and pick up his boarding pass. Puzzlingly enough for the surveillance team, he then drove back to his office instead of staying at the airport until his scheduled time of departure.

The reason became clear a couple of hours later when Regan drove back to the Courtyard Marriott and parked. By leaving his vehicle there, he wouldn't have to pay for parking at Dulles. He had made the earlier trip to the hotel to find out the pickup times of the Marriott's free shuttle service to the airport.

Before getting on the shuttle, Regan opened up the hood of the van. He took off his wedding ring and put it in the carburetor along with his car keys. Experience had taught him that the ring was a liability when it came to picking up women. The trip he was

Brian Patrick Regan, at about fifteen years of age, pictured in the 1977 Mill Lane Junior High yearbook.

FBI special agent Steve Carr, with his wife, Michelle.
Courtesy of Michelle Carr

All photos courtesy of the FBI unless otherwise noted.

FBI supervisory special
agent Lydia Jechorek.
Courtesy of Lydia Jechorek

ABOVE: FBI cryptanalyst Daniel
Olson.

RIGHT: FBI intelligence analyst
Marc Reeser.

TOP LEFT: FBI special agent William C. Lace.   *Courtesy of Dawn J. Langston*

TOP RIGHT: Bret Padres, an agent with the Air Force Office of Special Investigations, helped trace Regan's digital footprints on Intelink.   *Courtesy of Jill Padres*

BOTTOM LEFT: FBI special agent Kathy Springstead.
Courtesy of Treasured Images by Jeffrey, LLC

BOTTTOM RIGHT: Gary Walker, an agent with the Air Force Office of Special Investigations, was instrumental in helping to identify Regan as the prime suspect.
Courtesy of Bradley Wilson

FBI surveillance of Brian Regan visiting the Crofton library, where he conducted an Internet search for foreign embassy addresses on June 13, 2001.

In the FBI's video surveillance of Regan, he was seen writing into a spiral notebook at his NRO cubicle the morning of August 23, 2001. He was arrested later that day.

Brian Patrick Regan on the day of his arrest.

Account NR	B/A	Name	Credit Left	Date	where card	owe	
72004	A	Optima	1600.00	20 July	A wallet	16,453	325.00
6274	B	First usA Chevy Chase	170.00	20 July	B wallet	9 314	186.00
8880	B	First usA	200.00	5 Juny		4,300.00	86.00
3852	B	National city	100.00	15 Janney		6,898.00	135.00
1271	B	MBNA	Ø	20 July June		12,457.	281.00
7413	A	CHASe	1000,00	20 July		9,035	180.00
8487	B	wells FARgo	3000,00	20 July		1013	25.00
7762	B	National city	Ø	20 July		8 643	210.00
1710	A	Bank of America	0	20 may			
8254	B	Security Service	400.00	5 July		7563	95.00
5596	B	CHoice	-300.00	20 may		5635	117.00
13007	—	Optima	400.00	5 July		3,168	65.00
8970	B	Discover	0-7200	5 July Cancled		4.501	95.00
9033	B	CApital one	500.00 Cancelled	20 may			
9415	A	Firstusa	Ø	20 July		4 326	86.00
3092	A	CApital one mc	Ø -70.00	5 July 2001		430.00	30.00
3656	A	First usA	B 800.00	20 July 2001		3 422.	68.00
0932	A	PLATinum	Ø	July 20		1600.00	
5953		MBNA	Ø 100.00 (90.00)	20 July 20 June		9414.	

ABOVE: Regan kept a running tally of balances due on his numerous credit cards, but his financial state just kept spinning out of control.
Courtesy of the author

RIGHT: A cryptic note found in Regan's wallet at the time of his arrest.

MW-56NVOAIPG·CBIOIPG·tuS
VCt - AV-5333410117 93418
5S-CVOEFtQMBUA3CFSO-
5767952 188 37795

One of four sheets of trinomes Regan had in a folder he was carrying when he was about to leave Washington, D.C., for Europe on August 23, 2001. They turned out to be encrypted coordinates of sites in Pocahontas State Park, Virginia.

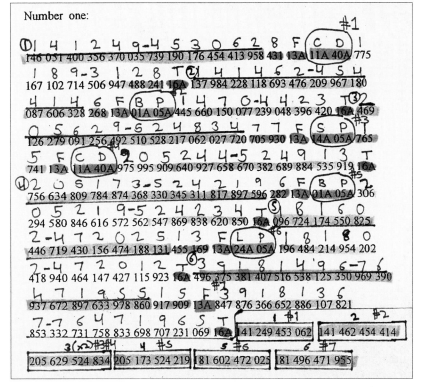

Regan's code for the burial sites in Patapsco Valley State Park in Maryland, marked up and decrypted.

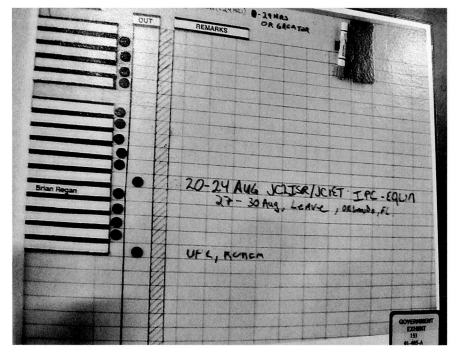

On a whiteboard in the NRO's Signals Intelligence Applications and Integration Office, Regan noted when he was going on leave to Orlando. In fact, he had planned to visit embassies in Europe to sell secrets.

Artist Dana Verkouteren's sketch of a moment from the first day of Regan's trial, January 27, 2003. Assistant U.S. Attorney Patricia Haynes made the opening arguments for the prosecution.   *Courtesy of Dana Verkouteren*

about to make wasn't just for espionage. He had another kind of betrayal in mind.

At Dulles, Lace and his fellow agents were waiting at the gate closest to the Lufthansa counter. They were all wearing uniforms bearing the logo of Argenbright—a company contracted to provide security at the airport. The plan was to whisk away Regan's carry-ons for a search when he came through. But Regan didn't show up, even though surveillance had seen him board the shuttle bus at the Marriott.

Carr met up with the team. He still hadn't received word on whether Regan was to be arrested or not. Carr's supervisor—Lydia Jechorek—had gone over to the Department of Justice to brief officials about the status of the investigation. Regardless of what the DOJ ended up deciding on the question of arresting Regan, the top brass within the FBI and the NRO had made up their minds not to allow Regan to leave the country.

To guarantee that, the government had taken an unusually rare step. In the hours prior, the State Department had issued a letter signed by Secretary of State Colin Powell revoking Regan's passport. Carr was carrying the letter in his pocket. He'd been instructed that it was to be used only as a last resort.

While Carr and the others waited anxiously at the gate expecting Regan to arrive at any minute, Jechorek was pressing her case at the Department of Justice. In the room was John Dion, a tall, wiry attorney in charge of counterespionage matters at the DOJ. The arrest had to be authorized by him.

Dion was an intense man in his sixties who had been involved in the prosecution of nearly every important spy case since the beginning of the Cold War. Jechorek had known him since 1985, when she investigated Jonathan Pollard, the naval intelligence analyst who was convicted of passing U.S. secrets to Israel. The first time Jechorek made Dion's acquaintance was when he took her to task for having arrested Pollard without authorization from the DOJ. Back then, she hadn't known the rules. This time, she had no such excuse.

It seemed simple enough: all she had to do was brief Dion on Regan and ask that the FBI be allowed to arrest him. There was a frustrating bureaucratic hurdle, though, that stood in the way. According to newly instituted rules at the DOJ, FBI agents weren't allowed to speak directly to officials in charge of making prosecutorial decisions. In matters related to national security, the bureau was required to go through the Office of Intelligence Policy and Review—the same office the investigators had approached when they wanted authorization to conduct surveillance on Regan.

The problem was that the head of OIPR, James Baker, was out for a few hours attending to some other official business. He was expected back by the middle of the afternoon, and Jechorek and the other FBI officials who had accompanied her had no choice but to wait. Meanwhile, Jechorek's cell phone kept ringing every few minutes. The person calling her was Anthony Buckmeier, a colleague of hers from the Washington Field Office who was supervising the operation at the airport.

"Did you get the authorization?" he asked.

"Not yet," Jechorek answered. "We're waiting for Jim Baker."

"What do you mean, you're waiting for Jim Baker?" The uncertainty was driving Carr and the other agents crazy, Buckmeier explained, dropping a few F-bombs along the way.

"I'll call you as soon as a decision is made," Jechorek replied, glancing at her watch for what seemed like the hundredth time.

To give itself some breathing room, the FBI had asked Lufthansa earlier that day to bump Regan to a later flight. The airline had obliged willingly, offering him a first-class seat on Flight 419, scheduled to leave at six fifteen. But now, even this extra time was dangerously close to running out. Not only were the agents vexed by the delay in decision making at the DOJ; they were also concerned that there was no sign of Regan with just over an hour to go before departure.

Then it dawned on Carr that Regan didn't necessarily have to come to the gate where the agents had positioned themselves. Since he'd collected his boarding pass earlier, he could go through security at the west end of the airport, which the Marriott's shuttle would have gotten to first. It was a simple detail that had been overlooked despite all the meticulous planning.

"Crap," Carr said. He scrambled toward the other gate, accompanied by an agent named Dave Lambert and two SWAT team members. By now, surveillance specialists were scanning the west end, and one of them spotted Regan going through security. By the time Carr and the others got to the concourse, Regan had stepped into a coach that was taking passengers to Terminal C, where his flight was to depart from.

"He's on People Mover Number Five," a surveillance specialist said on the radio, using the name the bus-sized vehicles were known by.

Carr could see Regan all the way at the back of the coach, his tall figure standing out in the crowd.

"Do not let this people mover move," Carr told the driver, who was standing out in the front.

"Who the hell are you?" the driver asked. He was about to close the doors.

Carr flashed his badge. "It's not going anywhere until you see me get off," he said.

"OK," the driver said, backing off.

Carr and Lambert stepped into the coach, which was jam-packed and as hot as a furnace. Outside, the runways shimmered under the hot August sun. Carr wished he hadn't worn a suit.

Carr didn't have the authorization to arrest, but he had the letter to revoke Regan's passport. It was now or never.

The two agents started making their way through the crowd. "Excuse me. Pardon me. Coming through," Carr said as they inched toward the back. Finally, the two men stood face-to-face with Regan.

"Mr. Regan," Carr said, holding up his badge. "I'm with the FBI. We have a couple of questions for you. Do you mind coming with us?"

Carr's voice was calm and friendly, but his mind was racing with anticipation. What would be the best move if Regan got physical? Carr visualized grabbing his baton and swinging it at the spy, but he wondered if there would be enough room in this crowd to do that without hitting anybody else.

Regan stared at Carr with a dazed expression, looking not the least bit menacing. Carr thought he looked like a teddy bear.

"Sure," he replied, picking up his duffel bag. The agents led him out of the coach and onto the concourse. Holding him by the elbow, they marched him into a room the FBI had arranged for the questioning.

The three men sat down at a table, Regan facing the two agents. All day, Carr had been agitated about not getting authorization to arrest Regan, but right now, he saw that indecision as a blessing.

It meant that Regan didn't have to be read his Miranda rights, improving the chances that he would submit to the interview. Carr's plan was to keep Regan talking for as long as possible, which was why he had asked the other agents not to knock on the door even if they got word from the DOJ. For no matter what the DOJ's decision was, Carr knew, it was likely to halt the interview.

"Why are you going to Germany?" Carr asked.

"Because I can," Regan replied. He looked relaxed.

"On business or pleasure?"

"Pleasure."

"What does your wife think?"

"Business." The answer was matter-of-fact.

"Do you know anything about code?" Carr asked.

"No," Regan said, unhesitatingly.

"Really?" Carr said. He slid a sheet over to Regan. It was the cover letter that was in each of the three packages mailed to the Libyan embassy. "Do you recognize this?"

Regan scanned the document. "I have no idea what this is," he said, looking up.

"What about this?" Carr asked, this time sliding over a copy of the alphabetic key found in the codebook sent to the Libyans.

Once again, Regan didn't flinch. He claimed not to have seen the document before.

"Am I going to be able to make my flight?" he asked. It was five fifteen p.m.

The agents didn't answer. There was a knock on the door. Duncan Wainwright, the chief attorney of the FBI's Washington Field Office, poked his head in.

"Can I talk to you, Dave?" Wainwright asked Lambert.

Wainwright hadn't been there earlier when Carr had instructed everybody not to interrupt the interview. In any case, Wainwright's job was to ensure that all the rules were followed, even if that conflicted with Carr's desire for an extended interview with the subject.

Minutes earlier, Jechorek had called from the DOJ and spoken to Tony Buckmeier, the supervisor in charge at the airport.

"We have authorization to arrest Regan," she had said. "About time," Buckmeier had replied. Wainwright conveyed the decision to Lambert outside the interview room.

A little later, Lambert came back in with a document in hand. "Brian, you know how government works," he said, casually. "We're going to have to get you to sign this advice-of-rights form." It was the equivalent of reading Regan his Miranda rights, except that it sounded like routine paperwork. Carr and Lambert made him initial every line, including one that read: "You may refuse to answer any question if a truthful answer to the question would tend to incriminate you." The formality over, the interview resumed.

Carr took out eight-by-ten glossy photographs of the sheets with trinomial numbers that agents had found in Regan's duffel bag that morning. He pushed them toward Regan.

"Can you tell me what this is?" Carr asked.

Regan looked down at it. His face fell.

"This is my stuff," he said, his voice wavering. Suddenly, he looked deflated, as if the air had been sucked out of him. "I think I need a lawyer."

The agents stood up and opened the door. "The interview is over," Carr told the agents outside. Wainwright walked into the room.

"Brian, you understand what's happening here," he said. "You are under arrest."

CHAPTER 7

DECIPHER THIS

C arr stared at the words in front of him.

Tricycle Lockpost Glove Motorcycle.

He read on.

Switch Weapon Pen Las Vegas.

Thirteen words in all, along with the curious notation "21month" scribbled sideways across the page of a spiral notebook that agents had found on Regan when they searched him after his arrest. Now, two days later, Carr sat in a large conference room at the Washington Field Office puzzling over what the innocuous string of words could possibly mean.

They made no sense, just like the four sheets of handwritten trinomes Regan had been carrying in his accordion folder. There were other seemingly nonsensical notes that agents had recovered from him. In his wallet, he had been carrying a three-by-five index card with twenty-six words that could have been randomly plucked out of a dictionary. Also found in the wallet was a piece of paper penned with a sequence of letters and numbers that looked like gobbledy-gook. The four lines on it began "56NVOAIP . . ." and ended with ". . . 18837795."

In Regan's checked-in brown suitcase, agents had found an assortment of things that to them seemed odd: a bag of sand, a Tupperware container, six plastic garbage bags, and a bottle of Elmer's glue. In the duffel bag, Regan was carrying a GPS. The list of puzzling possessions didn't end there. On the night of the arrest, after Regan was taken to the Central Virginia Regional Jail in Orange, Virginia— ninety miles from D.C.—a correctional officer had discovered, tucked between the inner and outer sole of Regan's shoe, a folded piece of paper bearing handwritten addresses in Europe. They turned out to be the addresses of the Iraqi and Chinese embassies in France, Switzerland, and the Netherlands.

Strange and inexplicable as these things were, they weren't incriminating. On their own, they didn't prove that Regan had committed espionage or that he'd even conspired to do so. There was nothing unlawful about writing down gibberish on sheets of paper, or hiding embassy addresses in one's shoe. Regan had also done nothing illegal by lying to his boss about where he was going, even though he might have technically violated a rule at his job requiring advance notification of foreign travel. The only sensitive information agents had found in his luggage consisted of a handful of NRO course descriptions—the same document he'd been seen creating at his office on August 15 by cutting out portions of an NRO course catalog. Regan had kept two copies of it inside a pornographic magazine he was carrying in his duffel bag; he had assumed, erroneously, that security officials would find it awkward to thumb through an X-rated glossy if they decided to search his luggage. While the courses were classified, the course descriptions were not, and so their value as evidence of an espionage plot was fairly limited.

Because of these reasons, the FBI had been compelled to mention the origins of the investigation in its criminal complaint against Regan, which Carr had helped to draft the day after the arrest. Without disclosing the source of the predicating information, the complaint laid out how the FBI—after learning that a number of classified documents had been provided to "the government of Country A"—had traced those documents to Regan's computer at the NRO. It went on to describe Regan's activities in the days and hours leading up to the afternoon of August 23, and listed the various materials seized from him, including the pages of trinomes—which were characterized as possible "handwritten encrypted messages"—and the GPS unit, which according to investigators could have been meant for locating a drop site. Based on these facts, the FBI's charge was that Regan had conspired to commit espionage against the United States.

But even though the complaint had relied on the intercepted packages to make the case against Regan, the agents and attorneys assembled in the conference room that morning knew that whatever had been handed to the FBI by the confidential informant was off-limits for the purpose of prosecution. As the group discussed its options, an uncomfortable question hung in the air. In the absence of alternate evidence, how could the government hope to prove the conspiracy charge?

Reviewing the items in front of him, Carr looked again at the spiral notebook. It looked familiar. In a video recording of Regan's work space from the morning of August 23, which Carr had had a chance to look at the day after the arrest, Regan was seen scribbling in a notebook that looked identical. It wasn't hard to tell that it was, in fact, the same notebook, because the video showed Regan writing sideways on the page. That's how the thirteen words had been penned in the notebook that Carr now had in front of him.

"What was he looking at when he wrote these?" Carr quizzed his fellow agents.

The answer wasn't hard to find—it was in the records of Regan's computer activity. Like most other days, Regan had logged in to Intelink within minutes of arriving at the office that morning. He was seen writing in the notebook while viewing an aerial image of the same Chinese missile launch facility that he'd looked at on August 15.

The Chinese military had been preparing the site for a test in prior weeks, and the United States had been monitoring the development through satellite reconnaissance. The image that Regan had looked at on the fifteenth had been photographed on August 9; the image he'd viewed on the twenty-third had been snapped two days earlier, on the twenty-first. The fact that spy satellites had taken at least two different pictures of the site within a two-week period showed how keen the United States was to follow what the Chinese were doing there.

"Thirteen words," Carr wondered, looking at the image. "What's on this page that is thirteen words?"

It struck him that the coordinates of the site—the digits of the latitude and longitude—added up to thirteen. Had Regan converted them into a code?

Just as Carr was mulling that over, an agent walked over to him with items that had been found in Regan's wallet. Among them was an AT&T calling card with a Post-it note stuck on the back. Written on it was Regan's Ameritrade account number, followed by the words "Hand Tree Hand Car."

By Carr's reasoning, each of the words on the Post-it represented a digit. Following a simple visual scheme, his guess was that "hand" stood for 5, corresponding to the number of fingers, "tree" represented 1, and "car" stood for 4.

Could 5154 possibly be the passcode Regan had set for his Ameritrade account? There was only one way to find out.

From the speakerphone on the conference table, Carr dialed Ameritrade's 800 number. He went through the prompts and entered Regan's account number. The system asked for Regan's passcode.

Carr punched in "5154."

There was silence around the table as Carr waited for the system to respond. The next couple of seconds seemed to go on forever. Then a recorded voice spoke up indicating that the passcode had been accepted.

In Regan's wallet, agents had found a second Post-it note with his IRA account number. Below it was another series of words that Carr took to be the passcode to access the IRA account. Carr decided to test his theory again. One of the words was "skate." Another was "stool."

"What could 'skate' mean?" he asked, looking around the room.

Somebody suggested 8—the number that skaters learn to carve on the ice as part of a popular figure-skating exercise. Carr thought it was a logical guess.

He debated whether "stool" represented 4 or 3. After all, some stools have four legs; others have three. Carr wanted to get it right on the first try. He was worried that the wrong passcode could get them locked out of the account, foreclosing the option of trying out any further guesses.

Given Regan's Irish background, Carr thought 3 was more likely. The classic Irish milking stool—used for sitting down by a cow's udder to milk it—has three legs, not four.

He called the number for Regan's IRA account and punched in the code he and the others had inferred. Once again, they got immediate access.

His hypothesis confirmed, Carr translated the thirteen words into digits, using the same pictorial logic he'd applied to crack the passcode. The first word in the string was "tricycle." Sure enough, it corresponded to 3, the first digit in the latitude of the missile site. "Lockpost" signified 1; "motorcycle" and "switch" represented 2; "weapon"—evocative of a revolver with six chambers—translated to 6. Although less obvious, the words "Las Vegas" and "casino" represented the number 7, by virtue of their association with gambling, evoking the reference to "lucky 7."

As the words fell into place one by one, fitting the coordinates perfectly, it became obvious to Carr and the others that Regan had adopted a strategy frequently employed by dyslexics: using images to remember text. The notation "21month" also became intelligible—it was a reference to the date, August 21, when the image of the missile site had been photographed.

When agents applied the same principle to the twenty-six words on the index card found in Regan's wallet, they got two sets of coordinates. One of them was of the same Chinese launch site, except that Regan had marked it with a different date—August 9— indicating when the United States had photographed the site previously. The other coordinates specified the location of a mobile Iraqi surface-to-air missile launch system in the northern no-fly zone, again photographed on a specific date that Regan had en-coded separately. Investigators realized that the index card was the same one Regan had been seen writing on a week before his arrest.

Now that they knew some of the information that Regan was planning to take with him to Europe, Carr and his fellow agents were in a position to make some definitive claims about Regan's intent that they felt could be backed up by evidence. The addresses hidden in his shoe suggested that he was planning to visit Iraqi and Chinese embassies to offer U.S. defense secrets. By sharing the coordinates of the two sites he'd encoded, the agents believed, Regan intended to prove his legitimacy and his access to top secret information.

Regardless of what secrets Regan may have followed up with, using those coordinates as a business card would have been enough to hurt the United States. Telling the Iraqis that the United States knew where one of their missile systems was located would en-courage the Iraqis to move the system to a new and possibly un-detectable site, making American planes patrolling the zone more vulnerable to attack.

On September 11, 2001, three weeks after Regan's arrest, Michael Gould turned on the TV at his home in Farmingdale and saw the horrifying images of airplanes crashing into the World Trade Cen-ter in Manhattan. Like millions of Americans, he was stunned by the unfolding tragedy of the attack. Then, as news arrived of a third plane having crashed into the Pentagon, Gould thought about Regan. The two hadn't talked in a while, but he recalled that Regan used to work at the Pentagon. "Oh my God, he could have been killed in this attack," Gould thought.

He picked up the phone and called Regan's house in Bowie. After hearing Anette's voice on the other end, he asked if Regan was OK.

"Oh, haven't you heard?" she said.

"What?"

"Brian's in jail."

"For what?" Gould asked, shocked a second time that morning.

"Treason," Anette said darkly.

"Get out of here," Gould said, incredulous.

"I can't believe it either," she replied.

Like the Twin Towers in Manhattan, Anette's world had come crashing down on the evening of August 23, when the FBI came knocking on her door. Agents spent hours searching the house, with police vans parked on the street, while Anette fought back tears and took care of the kids. When the agents left, they took with them boxes upon boxes of documents—everything from old financial records to letters—as well as Regan's two laptops. To Anette, the night had felt like a terrible dream.

In the days since, she had struggled to make sense of what the government was claiming about her husband. This wasn't the man she had known for the past nineteen years. When the two had first met, in the sunny Mediterranean, she was drawn to Regan because he seemed strong and stable, like her father. Over time, she had been forced to reconcile with his emotionally distant personality—perhaps the flip side of his apparent strength. At times, it seemed as if his feelings were locked up in an impregnable fortress. The trait made him reluctant to socialize and made it difficult for the couple to cultivate friendships. His aloofness had certainly not helped their marriage, especially after the first few years, and Anette had grown accustomed to the resulting bouts of loneliness that visited her with increasing frequency as the years went on.

Yet she also knew her husband to be kind and caring. He was the kind of person who would help old ladies cross the street. When he worked at the Pentagon, he had donated bone marrow to a leukemia patient who was a stranger to him. He sent money to charities to help feed starving children. How could a man like that commit espionage?

What she found most difficult to believe was the accusation that Regan had acted out of greed. The husband she knew—disappointingly enough for her—had never demonstrated a desire to be wealthy. When the kids demanded things they wanted—candy, toys, video games—he would often get irritated and lecture them on how there was more to life than the pursuit of material pleasures. Despite his impatience with the kids, she felt he had been a good father, joking around with them at home, taking them to the playground, and playing basketball with them. She liked that he took the kids to the library whenever he could and told them how important it was to read.

She was aware that he had financial worries—even though she herself was strangely detached from them—but she had never sensed any bitterness or resentment in him about not having enough money. Every now and then, he would remind her that they had a pretty good life. "Think of some of the other people out there," he would say. "Homeless people. People in other countries."

That's why the idea of his conspiring to betray the United States was confounding to Anette. True, Regan had never been one to wear his patriotism on his sleeve. But Anette knew him to be thankful for having been born in the United States. He'd mentioned to her how he hadn't always felt safe during visits to countries like Sudan and Egypt, trips that made him appreciate all the more the freedoms enjoyed by those living in the United States. Anette had always thought that Regan felt indebted to the military. He wanted his kids to join the services. Anette recalled that she had opposed the idea, but Regan had insisted that it was a great option for those who couldn't afford to pay for college. It was unfathomable to her that a man who recommended military service to his children could think of selling the secrets of that same military to a hostile government.

This had to be a mistake.

On October 23, 2001, a grand jury indicted Regan in the U.S. District Court for the Eastern District of Virginia on one count of attempted espionage. It was an unfortunate coincidence for him that the date happened to be his thirty-ninth birthday.

Unlike the criminal complaint, the indictment made no mention of the intercepted packages that had sparked the FBI's spy hunt. Instead, it cited Regan's prolific surfing of Intelink sites that didn't relate to his job, his search of Libyan embassy addresses at the Crofton library right before his trip to Europe in June, and the words in the spiral notebook and on the index card, which prosecutors charged were a "personal system of code" used by Regan to represent the coordinates of systems portrayed in classified images.

A week after the indictment, government prosecutors met with Regan's defense attorneys at the federal courthouse in Alexandria, Virginia. The meeting was initiated by the government under a proffer agreement, a standard practice in criminal law that allows defendants to provide information to the prosecution with the assurance that it won't be used at trial.

Most espionage investigations don't result in criminal charges, even when the government is convinced of wrongdoing. The reason is that the prosecution of spies—be they U.S. citizens or foreign agents operating in the United States—can involve the disclosure of intelligence-gathering methods and other sensitive information that the government would rather keep under wraps. When an investigation confirms that an individual is a spy, the government can choose to simply remove the person from a position of access—by taking away his or her secret clearance or, in the case of a foreign citizen, deporting the individual back to his or her home country. Even when an investigation does lead to a criminal complaint, more often than not, the person being charged ends up pleading guilty rather than going to trial.

That was the outcome prosecutors were hoping for when they met with Regan's attorneys. Leading the defense team was Nina Ginsberg, a tough, bespectacled woman who counted national security law among her specialties. This wasn't the first spy case for Ginsberg. Five years earlier, she had represented the FBI turncoat Earl Pitts, who was convicted of spying for Russia.

After all the paperwork had been signed, the discussion began. The lawyers on either side were no strangers to one another; their paths had crossed before. Ginsberg was especially familiar with Randy Bellows, the assistant U.S. attorney who had led the prosecution of Earl Pitts.

The atmosphere was cordial, but it was clear to the prosecutors from the beginning that Ginsberg intended to play hardball. She told them she didn't believe the government's case against Regan was very strong. Based on everything she'd learned about the investigation, she didn't think the FBI was prepared to furnish any evidence that Regan had contacted a foreign power.

Then Ginsberg dropped a bombshell. She disclosed that Regan

had hidden multiple packages of classified information in two separate geographical locations close to each other. "He's got stuff buried out there that could start a war," she said.

The words were a startling admission of guilt, but it was made in a proffer and hence useless for the purposes of prosecution. Randy Bellows and his fellow government attorneys knew that Ginsberg had made that statement to begin negotiations for a plea bargain. But they weren't prepared for what she was about to propose.

If the prosecution agreed to a prison term of less than nine years, Ginsberg said, Regan would help the government recover the documents. Otherwise, the government was welcome to try to find the packages on its own.

The prosecutors were stunned. It wasn't until after the meeting that they fully grasped the audacity of the offer. Regan was attempting to blackmail the United States government by holding hostage the secrets he had hoped to sell for cash. His release was the ransom he was demanding.

When Carr and his fellow investigators learned about Ginsberg's remark, they finally had confirmation of what they'd guessed all along. In Regan's letter to the Libyan embassy, he'd written about having removed and stashed eight hundred pages of classified documents. Now, after analyzing Regan's Intelink history as well as his badging records at the NRO, which showed the great frequency of his visits to the high-speed copier rooms where printers were located, agents speculated that the number of pages he'd taken was probably in the thousands.

Carr and his colleagues had also had prior reason to believe that Regan might have buried documents somewhere. Searching Regan's van, they had found several little pieces of paper and other pocket litter he'd emptied out in the vehicle, including a number of task lists he'd written for himself. Among them, the agents had discovered a curious note that began with the words: "Loc List." Below it was a host of cryptic words and numbers, such as:

> *Bear trail 369299—(4-5-6)*
> *Tennis Ball 365652-55*
> *A-Horror 32N-S beer bottle*

This was followed by a hyphenated string that the agents found repeated in various other notes as well:

> *Turkey-block-rugs 884 A—35steps-dirt-log-Mexican*

Puzzling over this and other notes, investigators had made some reasonable guesses. The "32N-S" most definitely seemed to be a reference to an exit sign near which Regan had pulled over while driving around in Farmingdale the weekend before his arrest. That's where surveillance specialists had seen Regan exit his vehicle and go off into the wooded area on the side of the road. It was consistent with "A-Horror"—a likely shorthand for the 1979 movie *The Amityville Horror* and therefore a reference to Amityville, which was one of the two towns named on the exit sign. Combined with the phrase "Loc List," which presumably meant "location list," the note suggested that Regan may have buried something in the woods next to the sign.

Agents had already searched that wooded patch. They had also looked around in the woods behind Farmingdale High School, where Regan had spent about fifteen minutes on that weekend trip.

They'd found a few items there—five cigars in separate Ziploc bags, a red Magic Marker—but none of them seemed relevant to Regan's conspiracy.

Although proffer statements cannot be used at trial, law enforcement agencies are free to rely on them to further their investigations. With the defense validating the theory that Regan had buried packages somewhere, what was until now a search for evidence turned into a hunt for stolen secrets. Carr and his team looked for clues in parks in Bowie that surveillance teams had seen Regan visiting with his dogs and kids. As winter approached, agents went back to his town house on Minetta Lane to conduct another extensive search. They checked every nook and cranny, knocking on air ducts and shining a flashlight inside the furnace while Anette looked on in sullen despair.

They found nothing.

While these searches were being conducted, top officials in the Justice and Defense Departments were deliberating on Regan's offer to help recover the secrets in exchange for a light sentence. One day in the late fall of 2001, they met at the U.S. Attorney's Office in Alexandria to discuss the matter. The chief counsels of the NRO and several other intelligence agencies were present in the room. Among the representatives from the FBI was Lydia Jechorek.

The counsels from the intelligence community were practically unanimous in wanting a deal. By now, the NRO's leadership had had a few weeks to estimate the potential damage that could be caused if the secrets Regan had stolen ended up in the hands of an adversary. The consequences would be nothing short of catastrophic, the agency had concluded, and so its top priority was to get the secrets back, no matter what it took. If that meant giving in to the demands of the very man who had caused the threat, then so be it. From the NRO's perspective, it was immaterial whether Regan got nine years or fifteen.

Jechorek's was one of the voices in the room to express strong disagreement with that view. She pointed out that Regan had researched past espionage cases in crafting his plan; future traitors would likely do the same. If the next insider to contemplate betraying the United States were to realize that Regan got a good deal because he was successful in hiding classified information, what would prevent that person from employing the same tactic? Jechorek asked. Accepting Regan's offer would solve the current crisis, but it would create a new hazard in the years to come: spies scheming to protect themselves through blackmail.

Jechorek's warning didn't fall on deaf ears. After further discussions, high-level officials in the Pentagon and the Justice Department concurred that the government would not submit to Regan's blackmail. Carr's team had to do everything it could to find the materials that Regan had hidden. The investigators realized that the key to tracing the documents likely lay in decoding the sheets with trinomes that Regan was carrying at the time of his arrest. So far, nobody had been able to make sense of them.

The use of codes for secret military and diplomatic communications dates back twenty-five hundred years. The Spartans are believed to have devised a simple cryptographic system known as a scytale as early as 400 BC, in which a strip of papyrus was wrapped around a staff like a ribbon to cover its entire length. The secret message was then written on this cylinder from one end to the other. In its unwrapped state, the text on the papyrus was meaningless, since the letters appeared in a nonsensical sequence. But when the receiver of the message wrapped it around a staff of the exact same diameter as that used by the sender, the message could be read out.

Centuries later, Julius Caesar used what may have been one of the first ciphers in history to correspond with military commanders and trusted aides. It involved shifting each letter in the message a certain number of places forward in the alphabet: if that number were 5, say, the letter *A* in "ARMY" would be enciphered as *F*, the next letter, *R*, as *W*, and so on.

Starting in the ninth century AD, Islamic scholars began systematically studying code making and code breaking. The philosopher Al-Kindi, born in what is now Iraq, birthed the field of cryptanalysis with his *Manuscript on Deciphering Cryptographic Messages*, written in the ninth century. In the treatise, he introduced a well-reasoned method for cracking a coded message without access to its key or cipher. In Al-Kindi's words, translated from the Arabic:

> *One way to solve an encrypted message, if we know its language, is to find a different plaintext of the same language long enough to fill one sheet or so, and then we count the occurrences of each letter. We call the most frequently occurring letter the "first," the next most occurring letter the "second," the following most occurring the "third," and so on, until we account for all the different letters in the plaintext sample.*
>
> *Then we look at the cipher text we want to solve and we also classify its symbols. We find the most occurring symbol and change it to the form of the "first" letter of the plaintext sample, the next most common symbol is changed to the form of the "second" letter, and so on, until we account for all symbols of the cryptogram we want to solve.*

The method described by Al-Kindi—now known as frequency analysis—went on to become a cornerstone of modern-day code breaking. Given that the making and breaking of codes is essentially a game of linguistic hide-and-seek, it's not hard to appreciate the principle behind Al-Kindi's approach. In every language, some letters and words are used more frequently than others, such as *E* and "the" in English. A coded message can often echo those frequency differences. Analyzing the relative number of occurrences of different characters in the encoded text can help figure out the rules used by the code maker to convert alphabets and numbers in the original message into gibberish. By the same token, a good code is one that provides no such statistical clues to the code breaker.

Starting in the thirteenth century, advances in mathematics helped drive the development of cryptography in Europe, where diplomats, administrative functionaries, and spies were increasingly using coded messages to secure their communications. Through the Renaissance years, as new and more secure ciphers were invented—among them the Vigenère cipher, which Brian Regan would use to encrypt his letter to the Libyans—cryptanalysts came up with techniques to crack them. By the nineteenth century, the use of cryptography had become commonplace in Europe and the United States.

With the birth of the telegraph, followed by the invention of the radio, encryption was no longer restricted to written communications. During Prohibition, from 1920 to 1933, rumrunners used coded radio messages to arrange the transfer of liquor from ships off the American coast to boats that would then smuggle the contraband ashore. The U.S. Coast Guard began intercepting and decoding these messages to determine the locations of the boats and capture them.

During the Second World War, the Axis and the Allied powers

spent an inordinate amount of effort on encryption and code breaking, which proved to be pivotal to the war's outcome. Working out of a research station called Bletchley Park near London, British mathematicians devoted themselves to cracking German messages that had been enciphered using Enigma machines—a typewriter-like devices with rotors and keys to convert plaintext into code and vice versa. In September 1940, around the same time that the British effort produced the first decryptions of Enigma messages, a team of U.S. Army code breakers cracked a Japanese diplomatic cipher called Purple. The UK's continued success in cracking Enigma ciphers, to which the Germans added complexity as time went on, and the United States' decryption of Japanese messages provided key intelligence to the Allies, helping to end the war sooner than would have been the case otherwise.

In the United States, the mission of decrypting foreign intercepts during World War II was led by the Signals Security Agency, which later became the National Security Agency. From 1943 to 1980, NSA cryptanalysts working on a secret program called Venona deciphered more than twenty-two hundred Soviet messages, many of them diplomatic communications. From these intercepts, the United States learned how the Soviet Union had attempted to steal the secrets of the Manhattan Project and identified a number of spies working in the United States on behalf of Moscow.

Through the decades of the Cold War, as cryptology became more advanced, the NSA increasingly relied on computer algorithms to break ciphers. By the 1990s, the focus of the NSA's cryptanalysis efforts had shifted from traditional code breaking to the creation and cracking of digital encryption systems. In the fall of 2001, however, when investigators requested the NSA's help in the Regan case, the agency's cryptanalysts were forced to revisit the basics of cryptography as they sought to make sense of Regan's trinomes. By the end of the year, with success nowhere in sight, the NSA called off the effort. The FBI assigned the task to one of the bureau's rising stars—a thirty-one-year-old cryptanalyst named Daniel Olson.

·

The son of Swedish immigrants, Olson grew up in a small town in central California, a cherubic kid with a round face, gray eyes, and blond hair. From his childhood up until his early twenties, Olson's life bore some striking similarities to the one Regan had lived, although he was eight years younger. He was the third of four kids, and the family—like Regan's—suffered dysfunction and discord because of his father's alcohol addiction. Olson didn't do nearly as badly at school as Regan did, but just as Regan struggled with dyslexia, Olson struggled with what he had come to accept as a severe, even if far narrower, handicap: the inability to do math. If he had sought medical help, he would possibly have received a diagnosis for dyscalculia, a dysfunction of the brain that makes it enormously difficult to perform arithmetic calculations and grasp math concepts.

Although Olson did not share Regan's problem of being perceived as unintelligent by friends and teachers, his difficulties with math were the source of a deep inadequacy that he felt throughout school and beyond. The last C he ever got in the subject was in third grade; from then on, it was consistently D or worse. It wasn't that Olson was incapable of mathematical reasoning—he did fine when it came to solving word problems. But numerical operations and formulas and equations—especially polynomial expressions—gave him mental paralysis.

The fear of disappointing his father—a tough man to please anyway—made Olson's math problem that much worse to handle.

Among other traumatic moments, he wouldn't ever be able to forget his last day in eighth grade, right before the family was to go on a trip to Disneyland, when he came home from school feeling mortified about how his father would react upon seeing that Olson had received yet another D in math. His mother, an artist with a far less exacting attitude toward academics, came to his rescue, by changing the D on his report card to a more respectable C.

Olson's family didn't have the money to support a college education, and Olson's grades weren't good enough for him to get a scholarship. Like Regan, he decided that the best option was to join the military. By doing so, he hoped also to win the approval of his father, who had served in the U.S. Army.

After enlisting in the National Guard and flunking math in community college, Olson joined active military duty in 1988. He was chosen to serve in Army intelligence, thanks to a demonstrated aptitude for pattern recognition, and ended up being sent to Goodfellow Air Force Base in San Angelo, Texas, to train as a signals analyst. Many of the courses he took there, including one on basic cryptanalysis, were those that Regan had taken years earlier. Olson discovered that he had a knack for code breaking. He later returned to Goodfellow for twelve weeks of advanced cryptanalysis training, during which he learned about an array of different ciphers and code systems, from those used in medieval wars to encryption schemes invented by Russian mathematicians during the 1920s and 1930s.

In the run-up to Operation Desert Storm in 1991, when Regan was helping to brief Air Force commanders on Iraq's missile defense, Olson was posted at a control center in charge of a handful of outstations eavesdropping on the Iraqi military. Iraq's battle units, keenly aware of the United States' signals intelligence capability, were doing their best to keep their radio communications to a minimum, and all that the outstations had picked up in several days of monitoring were a few stray snippets of conversation. It was impossible to extract any meaningful intelligence from them, but Olson noticed that the snippets were being heard around the same time every day.

Based on the pattern, Olson had all of the listening posts concentrate on one radio frequency during a window of time that he'd identified as the Iraqis' talking hour. The gambit paid off. Soon the Army was able to intercept a complete message.

Despite a fulfilling four years, Olson wasn't thrilled about continuing in the military. He left in 1992, got married, and started going to college for a degree in criminal justice. He found it difficult to get by without a monthly paycheck, however, and so a year later, he got a job as an analyst with a Drug Enforcement Agency task force in Savannah, Georgia, working during the day and taking classes in the evenings. Over the next few years, Olson came to specialize in tracking the use of UPS, FedEx, and other couriers by drug dealers to transport narcotics. Then, one day in 1996, a class he was taking as part of a money-laundering course reignited his interest in codes.

The class was being taught by a U.S. postal inspector, who was talking about how criminals use money orders to convert the proceeds from drug dealing into seemingly legitimate income. Covering an example, he asked the class to look at a money-order number that he projected on the screen. "Don't pay any attention to the last digit," he said. "It's coded and you can't figure it out anyway."

It was an offhand remark: since the lecture wasn't about codes, the inspector had no reason to go into them. But Olson, who was feeling bored, took it as a challenge and spent the next few minutes figuring out what the code could be. When he'd worked it out, he shared the answer with the person sitting next to him, who called it to the instructor's attention: "Hey, this military guy here broke your little code."

Annoyed at being interrupted, the instructor turned to Olson. "OK, smart guy, let's check it out," he said. Olson told him the steps he'd followed, and the instructor went through them on the board. It worked.

After the class ended, another instructor who had been sitting in the back of the room came up to Olson and introduced himself. The man's name was Eugene Saupp. He was a supervisor in a division of the FBI called the Racketeering Records Analysis Unit.

"Where did you learn to break codes?" he asked Olson.

"In the military," Olson replied.

Saupp gave Olson his business card and asked him to send him his résumé.

Less than a week later, he called Olson from Washington, D.C. "Hey, I don't have your résumé yet," he said.

A week later, Olson was on a plane to Washington, D.C., to interview for an analyst's job. He got the offer shortly after. The only thing he had to do before he could start was finish his undergraduate degree.

He couldn't tell Saupp or anybody else at the FBI why he didn't have the bachelor's under his belt yet. He'd failed to clear the required math courses, despite numerous attempts. Transferring from one college to another hadn't helped.

It was only with the help of an educational counselor that Olson managed to complete his undergraduate degree in the three months he had available, earning the math credits from a Savannah college where a particularly kind instructor helped him out with a C. In the spring of 1997, he started at the FBI, proud to report to work with his bachelor's degree in hand. Nobody asked to even look at it.

Although Olson had been hired for his code-breaking skills, he spent his first two years at the unit making sense of records seized from gambling syndicates and prostitution rings, which often use obscure and cryptic bookkeeping to protect their revenues and associates from law enforcement. In 1999, just as Olson was beginning to feel restless, he was handed a coded message that the Federal Bureau of Prisons had seized from an inmate. Members of prison gangs often use codes to communicate with one another.

Olson had never broken a code related to a criminal case before. What made the particular message doubly challenging for him was that it was in Spanish, a language that was foreign to him. After wrestling with it for a couple of days, he took it home for the weekend and sat down at the kitchen table with a Spanish dictionary beside him to check if he was on the right track. Late that night, when he thought he had solved it but couldn't find many of the decoded words in the dictionary, he called a military friend who knew Spanish. The friend recognized the words as slang. The message was a directive from one inmate to another commissioning a murder.

After that, Olson began getting drafted to break codes with increasing regularity. Within a year, he was doing code breaking full-time, working to decipher not just secret messages confiscated from prison gangs but also suicide notes and diaries of murder victims. Each of them was a challenge in some way or another, but as he would find out, none of them rivaled the complexity of the trinomes he was given in January 2002.

Olson talks fast and moves swiftly, as if his internal rhythm were just a little quicker than everyone else's. In his office at the FBI Laboratory in Quantico, Virginia, the shelves are lined with videotapes of Hollywood crime thrillers, some of which—like *Manhunter*—feature code making and code breaking in the plot. A display cabinet showcases relics of cryptography such as an Enigma machine from World War II. On his desk, he keeps a jar of peanuts and a box of graham crackers to sustain himself through stretches when he's too engrossed with problem solving to break for lunch.

In the first few weeks of 2002, Olson found himself having to replenish that stash of snacks constantly as the Regan papers consumed his every waking hour. Besides the handwritten materials seized from Regan at the time of his arrest, Olson had before him thirty sheets with similarly cryptic writings that jail authorities had recovered from Regan's cell during a series of routine jailhouse searches in November 2001. Regan had claimed he was preparing these papers in jail for his defense and that they were meant for his attorneys.

On first glance, the writing on some of these documents looked almost identical to the four sheets of trinomes. They were labeled similarly—S234, M341, M123456—and contained rows upon rows of three-digit numbers. In another document, Regan appeared to have created word puzzles, writing a series of jumbled spellings for words like "towel" and "Jesus." On some of the papers, he had scribbled numerical computations, multiplying, adding, and subtracting various numbers. One document, labeled "European Hunt," was a letter apparently to his kids providing clues for locating treasures he had buried for them. What was particularly baffling about this supposed treasure hunt was that the clues in it referenced missile sites in China and the Middle East. Regan had even picked the same missile types that he'd looked up on Intelink—CSS and SAM—in setting up the elaborate riddle.

It wasn't immediately clear to investigators what Regan was up to. Was he writing coded messages for a foreign agent? That seemed unlikely since he'd made no special effort to conceal the papers in his cell. The ease with which the prison staff had found them on four different searches from mid- to late November made Carr and his fellow agents wonder if Regan wanted the new materials to be discovered.

Olson compared the trinomes found in Regan's folder with those Regan had generated in prison. He noticed a couple of key differences between them. In the originally seized trinomes, the second digit was always a number ranging from 1 through 5, and the third digit was always 1 or 2. The prison trinomes, on the other hand, didn't follow that rule—the second and third digits could be any number ranging from 0 to 9. Further, in the original set of trinomes, some of the numbers had been crossed out and written over, and some appeared to have been corrected. There were no such errors in the prison trinomes. The difference suggested that the trinomes seized at the airport were not random. They were somehow more meaningful than the ones Regan had produced in his jail cell.

Next, Olson compared the two sets using statistical analysis. For each of the papers with the trinomes—including the four sheets from Regan's folder, marked "letters," and a total of six messages from the cell—Olson looked at what's known as an "index of coincidence," or IC. A mathematical tool invented by the legendary American cryptologist William Friedman—whose team cracked the Japanese diplomatic cipher Purple—the IC is a measure of the randomness of a text. It indicates the likelihood of finding the same character in the same position when comparing two units of a text side by side. Since such "coincidences" in an enciphered text can reflect an underlying pattern in the plaintext, calculating the IC of a coded message can help cryptanalysts find clues to breaking it.

Tabulating the ICs for the various documents, Olson could see a distinct difference between the two sets. There was a higher degree of randomness in the trinomes recovered from the cell. More important, the randomness for the first, second, and third digits varied widely between the six sheets of prison trinomes. By contrast, not only did the original trinomes exhibit less randomness in their digits; the extent of randomness was nearly identical for all three "letters."

The three "letters" had been encrypted using a common scheme, Olson concluded from the analysis. He was also convinced that the prison trinomes were dummy codes. They were meaningless. Regan's purpose behind generating them, investigators realized, was to make the original trinomes look like a game. It was a ploy to alter the evidence by adding noise to the signal.

That insight, however, didn't bring Olson any closer to cracking the trinomes that mattered. He researched the cryptanalysis literature to determine which encryption systems use three-digit numbers with the characteristics of the nearly three hundred trinomes contained in each of the three documents: Letter M-I134, Letter S-I134, and Letter A-341I. Since every trinome ended in 1 or 2, Olson was drawn to the possibility of a book code, in which the last digit of every number potentially referred to the first or second column of a printed page. The hypothesis seemed all the more plausible, as Regan was carrying a pocket dictionary in his duffel bag when he was arrested. Like most dictionaries, this one was printed in a two-column format.

Book codes—codes based on a book known to both sender and recipient—have been favored by spies in history because they can be nearly impossible to break, unless the book that holds the key has been identified. During the American Revolution, the American traitor Benedict Arnold wrote coded letters to the British Army in which each word was represented by a set of numbers indicating the page, line, and specific position where that very word would be found in an agreed-upon book. The ones Arnold chose were *Commentaries on the Laws of England,* by William Blackstone, and Nathan Bailey's *Dictionary.* During World War II, German agents in Egypt used Daphne du Maurier's *Rebecca,* a 1938 novel, as the basis of a code for transmitting intelligence from Cairo to support a campaign by the Axis powers against the Allies in North Africa. The discovery of the book among the possessions of two German radio operators who didn't read English ultimately led to the breaking of the code, which in turn led to the capture of the German spies in Cairo.

Olson flipped through Regan's dictionary. On one of the introductory pages, Regan had written "26MM" and "28SS," which to Olson appeared to be a reference to the letters with the trinomes. Throughout the dictionary, he found words that had been underlined or marked with a dot, most of them words rarely used in everyday conversation, such as "marsupial," "masochism," "pestilence," and "occident." Olson wondered if Regan had chosen the words as keys for his encryption scheme. But when he tested the idea in different ways, it didn't unlock any doors. Forensics experts examined the dictionary, as well as a novel that Regan had with him, for possible clues. They looked for Regan's fingerprints to determine which pages he'd looked at the most. They scanned the pages under a special light to search for anything written in invisible ink.

The scrutiny yielded nothing. After weeks of trying, Olson was out of ideas. For the first time in his career, he was prepared to concede defeat.

Frustrated by the trinomes, Olson focused his attention on another puzzle: the note from Regan's wallet containing a string of letters and numbers. It began "56NVOAI . . ." He had a hunch that it may have been enciphered using a Caesar shift—a method in which all the characters of a message are shifted by a fixed number of positions along the alphabet. He lined up the text on a slide board and shifted the letters by one place, two places, and so on, checking the other end of the slide board each time to see if he got anything readable.

After twenty-five shifts down the alphabet—it would have taken just one shift in the opposite direction—the first line of the text, "56NVOAIPG . . . ," resolved to "45 MUNZHOF BANHOF STR," which sounded like German. Plugging the result into YellowPages.com, Olson found that it was the address for the Swiss bank UBS in Zurich. The second line broke out to Bundesplatz 2 in Bern, the address for another Swiss bank. Both addresses were followed by a string of numbers that resolved to the latitude and longitude of the two locations.

Why Regan was carrying those addresses wasn't clear, but the fact that he'd concealed them using code could potentially help the prosecution build its case. It was a small consolation to Olson that he'd been able to break one of Regan's codes, albeit a simple one. But Olson's work on the case was far from over.

One day in early February, Regan's attorney, Nina Ginsberg, stopped by the office of Randy Bellows, the prosecutor in charge of the case. She had a simple question. Was the government planning to use anything from the Gateway laptop seized from Regan's house as evidence?

There was nothing unusual about the inquiry. It's common for the defense and the prosecution to consult with each other and define the scope of an impending trial by reaching a consensus on certain aspects of the case before stepping into the courtroom. By settling questions such as whether the prosecution intends to introduce something as evidence, or if the defense plans to challenge the credentials of an opposing witness, both sides can limit unnecessary effort and expense in preparing for trial and focus on the core dispute to be resolved before a jury.

Bellows knew that the FBI had examined the hard disks of a Toshiba and a Gateway found at Regan's house on the day of his arrest. Agents had learned that both laptops were pilfered from the NRO—Regan had removed the government stickers on them and scratched out their serial numbers—but their hard disks hadn't yielded anything of evidentiary value. It also became clear in the course of the investigation that Regan had been using primarily the Gateway; the Toshiba was used almost entirely by his kids. So when Ginsberg put her question about the Gateway to Bellows, he replied that the government wasn't planning to introduce any evidence from either of the laptops.

Following up with Bellows the next day, Ginsberg asked the same question a second time, just to make sure she'd understood him correctly. On Friday, February 8, she stopped by his office once again to raise the matter. This time, she asked if the prosecution could stipulate that the Gateway would be excluded from the case.

Not only was Bellows irritated by Ginsberg's doggedness; he also found it curious. He declined her request. Although the prosecution currently had no plans to introduce the laptops at trial, he told her, the government wasn't going to foreclose the option in case investigators found any evidence on them in the future.

As soon as Ginsberg had left, Bellows picked up the phone and called Carr. "Can you come over to my office right now?" he asked.

It was three in the afternoon when Carr drove from the

Washington Field Office to the federal courthouse in Alexandria to meet with Bellows and James P. Gillis, who at the time was a senior trial attorney with the internal security section at the Department of Justice.

"Did you find anything on the computers?" Bellows asked.

"No," Carr said.

"Are you sure about that?" Bellows wanted to know.

"Yes. Why?" Carr asked.

Bellows explained that Ginsberg had been inquiring about the Gateway repeatedly.

To double-check, Carr called Andrea Price-Lace, an agent from the bureau's Computer Analysis and Response Team—the group responsible for collecting and processing digital evidence.

"Andrea, I'm with Randy Bellows right now," Carr said. "Tell me something—did you all find anything on the hard disks?"

Price-Lace told him that her team had indeed run searches on the hard disks for a set of "dirty words" provided by the investigators—words like "top secret" and "classified." However, she explained that it wasn't CART's job to go through the results. That was left to the investigators.

Carr was flabbergasted. He'd been under the impression that CART had combed through the hard drives and failed to find anything. The assumption was based on his experience working on the investigation of the CIA traitor Jim Nicholson in the mid-nineties: one of the breakthroughs in that case had come when CART analysts found fragments of classified documents relating to Russia on Nicholson's notebook computer. However, CART's operating procedures had changed in the years since. Carr evidently didn't get the memo.

What this meant was that although six months had passed, Regan's laptops hadn't really been examined. Whether it was anybody's fault was beside the point. What mattered was that there had been a screwup and it needed to be remedied immediately.

On the drive back to his office, Carr called Jechorek, his supervisor. "Who's still in the bull pen?" he asked anxiously, expecting that many in the squad had left for the day. After all, it was late afternoon on a Friday.

"Everybody's here," Jechorek answered, to his relief.

"Don't let anybody go home," Carr said.

When he got to the office, he found in his desk drawer the DVDs that CART had made from searching and imaging the laptops. He and the other agents on the squad popped the disks into their desktops and began scrolling through the contents. CART had included the results of the dirty-word searches on the disks, which showed that some of the words had indeed been found. But it was impossible to tell where those words resided, and in what context.

The imaged files added up to more than 120,000 pages of text, the bulk of which was machine language. Pressing the "page down" button, the agents scanned the sea of characters on the screen for anything intelligible. Less than ten minutes after they'd begun, Carr let out a loud exclamation.

"Holy shit!"

The fragment of text that he was looking at read:

dA<J@P"dAK@P$dAK@P&dAL@P9dALM@P*dAN@ PdAN@P0dAO@P2dATP@P4dAQ@P6d@Q@@i@GEc: Times New Roman5VESymbol3&Ec:Arial"qeh!Flflf14x- o!20do@!R I AM A MIDDLE EAST, NORTH AFRICA ANALYST FOR THE CENTRAL INTELLIGENCE AGENCY (CIA) Valued Gateway Customereric33A: I-LETTER-SSdoca . . .

The sentence embedded in that string of nonsensical text was one that Carr would have recognize in his sleep. It was the opening of the cover letter Regan had included in the three envelopes he'd mailed to the Libyan embassy.

Excited, the agents kept scrolling through the pages, their eyes glued to their desktop screens. As afternoon rolled into evening, the silence of the bull pen was broken time and again by exultations accompanying new discoveries. Not only did Carr and the others come across more fragments of the cover letter; they also found the entire plaintext and enciphered versions of the letter in which Regan had spelled out his espionage offer to Libyan president Muammar Gaddhafi. There was also a cover letter written to Iran.

Along with that, the agents found an identical offer to the Iraqi president, Saddam Hussein. Carr had long suspected that Regan might have contacted countries other than Libya. Here was proof that the master sergeant had, at the very least, planned on contacting the Iraqi government with the intent of selling secrets.

All of these texts were in the slack space of the Gateway—the unallocated space on a computer's hard drive that users don't see on their screens. Regan had clearly used the laptop to type the letters and then deleted them, taking the standard precaution of emptying the recycle bin to satisfy himself that the documents were now completely erased.

What he didn't realize was that deleting a file on a computer doesn't necessarily get rid of the data. It remains on the machine, occupying the same space on the hard drive as before, except that the file name disappears from the directory and the data is now no longer sacrosanct. The computer's operating system now has permission to overwrite the old data with new data. In the case of the documents that Regan had deleted, the data was never overwritten.

At seven p.m., Carr called the prosecuting attorneys to give them the news. The evidence that the investigators had been trying to unearth for months had been lying in his desk drawer all along. Without a prod from the defense, the prosecution may well have remained ignorant about it.

The discovery of the letters on the Gateway strengthened the government's case against Regan, eliminating the need to introduce the envelopes mailed to the Libyan embassy as evidence. On February 14, 2002, less than a week after the breakthrough, a grand jury returned a superseding indictment against Regan, charging him with three counts of attempted espionage—on behalf of Libya, Iraq, and China—and one count of gathering national defense information.

Regan's letters to Gaddhafi and Hussein, disclosed in the indictment, incensed an American public still reeling from the shock of the 9/11 terrorist attacks. To many, his words looked like the very definition of treason. In Farmingdale, Regan's old friend Brian Wagner—who like many others had missed the news of Regan's arrest—was shocked when he read about the indictment. He called Bob Florio, the classmate who used to give Regan hell on his paper route, and began reading out the article on the phone in a tone of disbelief. When he got to the end of the article, however, he couldn't help chuckling. "Here's the kicker, where you know it's got to be Regan," Wagner said, proceeding to read out the part that mentioned that the letters discovered on the computer were filled with spelling errors.

The four-count indictment was bad enough, but things were about to get even more dire for Regan. In his State of the Union address on January 29, 2002, President George W. Bush had identified Iraq—along with Iran and North Korea—as part of an "Axis of Evil" that represented a grave threat to the United States and the rest of the world. The speech would later come to be seen as the first drumbeat of war against the Saddam Hussein regime. In that climate of hostility between the United States and Iraq, Regan's ploy to extort a lesser sentence for his treason by withholding the secrets he had stolen made officials in the Defense and Justice Departments furious. Here was someone who had not only conspired to commit espionage against the United States, but was now threatening the lives of U.S. servicemen, including pilots engaged in policing the northern no-fly zone in Iraq. By refusing to disclose where he'd stashed top secret national defense information— the extent of which was as yet unknown—he was in effect thumbing his nose at the American flag. If there was anything worse than treason, it was this.

Through the early weeks of spring, with Regan yet to make any offer of disclosure, decision makers in the government hardened their stand. The Department of Justice authorized the prosecutors to pursue the death penalty. It was the first time since the execution of the Rosenbergs in 1953 that the government would be seeking death for an alleged spy. Although such a decision had never been made before in an attempted espionage case, the prosecution was convinced that Regan's crime met the statutory requirements for a death-penalty trial.

The task of drafting the prosecution's notice to seek the death penalty fell on Gillis, who had moved from the DOJ to become an assistant U.S. attorney in the Eastern District of Virginia. His wife was vehemently opposed to capital punishment. In the months prior, when Gillis had told her that he had been assigned to work on a spy case, she had asked him pointedly if the case would involve the death penalty. He had never imagined that it might. "No, don't worry," he had told her. "It's attempted espionage."

Now, much to his discomfort, he found himself laying out the government's rationale for why death was a suitable punishment for Regan. Besides creating a "grave risk of substantial danger to national security" and a "grave risk of death" to another person—two aggravating factors cited under the death-sentence statute in federal law—Gillis argued that Regan's betrayal qualified for the death penalty on several nonstatutory counts. Unlike spies who had been convicted of passing one piece or several small pieces of classified information, Regan had sought to give away a broad sweep of secrets. He'd targeted multiple countries, pioneering what the prosecutors termed "form letter" espionage, in effect multiplying the potential risk to the United States. What made his crime particularly worthy of capital punishment, Gillis noted in the notice, was that Regan had used the death penalty as a marketing tool in his offer letters to demand the price he wanted. "If I am caught," Regan had written, "I will be enprisoned [sic] for the rest of my life if not executed for this deed."

Although officials would never admit it, the government's decision to seek the death penalty was as much a move to give exemplary punishment to a traitor as it was a negotiating tactic. Officials at the NRO were desperately anxious to recover the secrets Regan had stolen. The agency had conveyed to the Justice Department in no uncertain terms that the NRO's priority was to undo the damage Regan had caused. After Gillis had drafted the notice, he spoke to Regan's defense attorneys to impress upon them that their client still had the option to plead guilty. The offer on the table was that prosecutors would agree to seek a twenty-five-year prison sentence if Regan returned everything he had taken. It was his last chance,

Gillis told the defense. "Once we file the death-penalty notice," he said, "all bets are off."

Regan was given a few days to consider the offer, but he refused to budge. He seemed oblivious to the gravity of the situation, which had only worsened after the discovery of the letters on the laptop. He was still insistent that he be given a much shorter sentence. As he would later explain to a government-hired psychiatrist, "I'd take the death-penalty option rather than taking twenty years and missing out on my children."

On April 19, 2002, the prosecution filed the death-penalty notice in court. When Gillis told his wife about it, she reacted with shock and anger. Over the next several weeks, she told him more than once that she did not want to be sleeping next to a killer. Gillis, for his part, did his best to explain why the government believed Regan deserved to die. The man had hidden secrets that he could, in theory, still pass on to enemies of the United States. If he wasn't going to reveal where those secrets were, the government had no choice but to put him to death. It was a perfectly logical argument, but Gillis knew, even as he made it, that his wife was never going to be persuaded.

CHAPTER 8

A CONVOLUTED COVER-UP

Regan had thought a lot about death, long before he set out to commit espionage. He was convinced he was going to die young. Starting in his mid-thirties, he had been suffering frequent bouts of abdominal pain that made him worry that he had cancer. Somehow it had never occurred to him that his binge drinking and constant imbibing of Mountain Dew could be the cause of the problem. Even though doctors he'd consulted with never suspected cancer, he wasn't entirely convinced.

Natural death wasn't the only kind of death Regan had thought about. He had also wondered whether he was predisposed to mental illness that could drive him to suicide. The thought had established itself firmly in his mind after two of his maternal uncles—one in Ireland and one in the United States—killed themselves. Another of his mom's siblings—her sister—had died mysteriously at an elder-care facility, leading Regan to suspect that she, too, may have committed suicide. And so, he had come to ask himself: could some of the genes he shared with these troubled individuals lead him to one day engineer his own demise?

As he sat in his prison cell, those thoughts had come close to becoming a self-fulfilling prophecy. One day in the fall of 2001, a few weeks after his arrest, Regan had repeatedly banged his head against the wall, expecting to give himself a brain injury that he hoped would lead to death. The guards had stopped him well before he could hurt himself seriously.

As far as suicide attempts go, it was a pretty halfhearted one. As Regan would explain later, the head banging was intended to make the hoped-for death look like an accident. If it were declared a suicide, he had reasoned, his wife and children would be deprived of his life insurance. Like some of Regan's other plans, this one, too, seemed to have been doomed by overthinking.

Barring this incident, after which doctors put him on Prozac, Regan kept up his stoic exterior in prison. When Anette visited him every week at the Alexandria Detention Center, the two sat on opposite sides of a glass divider, talking through a phone line. The conversations were monitored by an FBI agent seated next to Anette. A device hooked up to the phone line recorded the talks. There was very little warmth exchanged during these calls, and though the two sat only a few feet across from each other, the monitoring agents could sense the emotional gulf that lay between them. Anette frequently expressed her bitterness and anger, which seemed to be directed at the government and her husband in equal measure. She ranted about how her life and the lives of their children had been upended by the investigation, how the numerous searches of their home had turned their lives into a nightmare. "I can't believe the government is doing this," she would say with disgust.

By contrast, Regan never raised his voice or showed any signs of agitation. At times, he seemed close to being catatonic. He had told her—as well as his parents and his sisters—that the government was making a mountain out of a molehill, that it was all a big conspiracy. At one point, he told them that the FBI was making him a scapegoat for the September 11 attacks. Anette didn't ask any questions to probe his vague and evolving defense. Whether it was out of a desire for self-protection or out of sheer naïveté, she showed no signs of venturing out of denial.

What she was most worried about was money. She had begun working and taking nursing classes, but raising four kids without Regan's income was a frightening prospect. Yet, as in the years before, the magnitude of the crisis seemed to elude her. In many of the conversations with Regan, monitoring agents heard her go on and on about Aztero, the stallion she had purchased from Sweden in the summer of 2001. She would complain about how she'd had no time lately to go visit the horse. She was paying $250 a month to a stable near Bowie for Aztero's upkeep, and though months had passed since Regan's arrest, she was still debating whether it was a good idea to sell the horse or to keep paying for its maintenance.

In the middle of one such conversation in September 2002, Anette said something completely out of context with the rest of their discussion.

"I'm knitting a sweater for Jamie,"* she said.

Regan responded with a nod.

The exchange was odd, but innocuous enough not to draw the attention of the agent monitoring the conversation. Its significance would elude the FBI until later that fall.

---

*The name was actually that of the Regans' youngest child, which I've changed to protect the child's identity.

At around nine a.m. on Saturday, October 12, shortly after inmates at the Alexandria Detention Center had finished breakfast, a deputy sheriff named Gregory Kimble walked down a corridor on the fourth floor of the jail building to conduct a routine search. Kimble was an old hand at performing these searches, which were part of a system of fortnightly "shakedowns" aimed at confiscating any drugs and weapons hidden by prisoners at the facility. He made it a point to check the utility closets between cells, knowing that inmates liked to stash contraband there.

That morning, when Kimble peeked into the utility closet adjoining Regan's cell, 4B-3, he noticed a couple of toilet paper holders sticking out of a hole cut in the wall for the cell's plumbing. Rolled up inside the holders were five or six handwritten pages. Some of the content seemed to have been written in code. It was obvious that Regan had hidden the pages there, sticking them in from the other side of the hole, which lay just below his sink.

Kimble confronted Regan, who told him that the papers were intended for his lawyers. When Kimble walked him over to a table outside the cell and asked him to mark the pages as "attorney-client material," Regan suddenly snatched the documents, ran back into his cell, and flushed them down the toilet.

Kimble and the other guards present rushed over to him, but it was too late. When they'd recovered their wits, one of them asked Regan, "What will you do about the copies we made?" The color drained from Regan's face when he heard the question, and he sat down on his bunk, saying nothing.

The truth was that the jail staff hadn't copied the documents.

They were hoping the scare would get Regan to tell them what he had been hiding and why. The ploy didn't work, though, and Regan eventually caught on to the guards' bluff. Since the materials were meant for his defense, he argued, the government had no business knowing what they were.

When the FBI received word of the incident, Carr and his fellow investigators were alarmed. From Kimble, who was able to recall fragments of text from his brief perusal of the pages, the agents learned that the message included instructions for ripping up the documents and flushing them down the toilet after their contents had been read. They didn't find it at all believable that Regan had written them for his lawyers. It was far more likely that he was planning to communicate with another party, perhaps even a foreign agent. Had he succeeded?

The suspicion led the FBI to investigate whether Regan had made an attempt to transmit anything out of prison unbeknownst to jail authorities. Agents reviewed his purchases at the prison canteen, where Regan spent most of his money buying Cheetos and other junk food. He had also bought a few stamped envelopes over the prior months. When the agents compared the tally of envelopes he'd purchased with the number of letters they knew he had mailed—all of which had been copied and reviewed by the FBI—it became clear that he had succeeded in sending out mail that circumvented the FBI's monitoring.

Interviewing others at the prison, agents found out that Regan had attempted to use other inmates on his floor to mail letters on his behalf, offering to have money deposited into their canteen funds. Two of the inmates had turned him down, but one had agreed to help in exchange for a payment of $5 every week, along with a promise of $500 to be paid when Regan got out of prison. Regan had slipped the letter to him inside a newspaper, which inmates were allowed to exchange freely. The person the letter was addressed to was Anette Regan.

To have FBI agents show up at her doorstep had become routine for Anette by the fall of 2002. In the year that had passed since Regan's arrest, her reaction to these intrusions had gone from shock to anger to sneering contempt. In her exchanges with agents during searches of the house, she never missed a chance to convey how stupid the FBI was for wasting its time on this wild-goose chase. She simply didn't believe her husband was capable of plotting the conspiracy he was being accused of.

And so when investigators rang her doorbell on the evening of November 1, Anette let them in with her characteristic sullenness, bracing herself for yet another search. Under different circumstances, she might have felt embarrassed about how disheveled the house looked, with the carpeting torn up, nail strips poking dangerously out from the exposed floor, piles of laundry everywhere and dishes stacked up in the sink, dust and dog hair all over. But her days of fretting over home maintenance were now well past. She had four children to support and take care of in her husband's absence; keeping the household running was enough of a struggle.

When the visitors told her they'd come to talk to her, she was taken aback. She led them in through the living room, her annoyance giving way to anxiety. "What do you want to know?" she asked.

A young agent named Kathy Springstead inquired if Regan had sent her a letter recently.

"Yes," she replied hesitatingly.

Springstead asked if she could hand it over. Anette walked over to a china cabinet in the dining room and returned with the letter. "I want to get this straightened out," she said.

Springstead and another agent sat down with Anette at the dinner table. In the eight-page letter, written by hand, Regan had explained to Anette how the FBI was trying to frame him. The letters that investigators claimed to have found on his computer had been planted, he wrote, because the FBI, after having spent so many resources on the case, was desperate to prove that he was a spy. Besides loading the letters onto the laptop's hard drive, he went on, the agents had taken another sinister step. They had removed the evidence that could prove his innocence.

Before he was arrested, Regan wrote in the letter, he had been burying toys and magazines at various locations as part of a treasure hunt he'd been creating for the kids. Those buried items were key to his defense, he explained, because they could prove that the materials he had with him at the time of his arrest—the GPS, the shovel, the handwritten sheets—had nothing to do with espionage. But he was convinced that the agents had dug up these innocent "treasures," he wrote in the letter, which was why he needed Anette's help to "re-create" his defense ahead of the trial.

He wanted her to go out to four locations in Maryland and Virginia and bury some innocuous objects from the basement— collectible drinking glasses bearing cartoons and magazines and comic books that he'd collected since the seventies. He asked that she wear gloves before handling the items, so as to leave no fingerprints, and wrap them up into packages. To make the packages look like they'd been in the ground for a while, he suggested leaving them in a mud bucket for a few hours.

The letter included maps for where he wanted them buried: in a wooded area by a horse barn in Crownsville—where Anette sometimes went to ride—and at a spot near the Rosecroft Raceway in Fort Washington. The maps were surprisingly detailed, despite having been drawn from memory. At the Crownsville location, for instance, Regan had sketched where Anette was to bury the toy relative to a fence near the riding trail. In Virginia, he directed her to a location near the NRO and another in Manassas Battlefield Park. Throughout the letter, Regan emphasized how important it was for Anette to be discreet and throw off FBI agents who were likely to be surveilling her. One suggestion he had for her was that she take the dog along for a walk: when she bent down to dig, he wrote, it would look like she was picking up poop. His other idea was that she take his sneakers along to pack down the dirt after burying each item: that would leave behind his footprints.

Springstead—allergic to pet dander—sneezed and sniffled as she took in the contents of the letter. All the dog hair around the house was playing havoc with her sinuses. "Are you OK?" Anette asked, more than once. It was the first time that the agents had seen her show any softness toward them.

They asked her if she had done what Regan had asked.

She told them she had, in fact, in two trips over the span of a month, buried some items at the two sites in Maryland. She hadn't had time to visit the other locations yet. In the letter, Regan had instructed her on how she could communicate to him—through code—that she'd carried out the given task. As Springstead would find out later from listening to recordings of the couple's conversations, Anette had done that by making that puzzling remark about knitting "a sweater for Jamie."

It was late in the evening when the agents wrapped up the interview. The next day, Springstead drove out with Anette to the sites that Regan had indicated in his letter, which the FBI wanted to search in order to verify Anette's story. In the car, Springstead attempted to strike up a conversation with Anette, whose indignation hadn't lessened one bit despite her admission. She didn't really comprehend why Regan had asked her to bury the toys; she told Springstead the story of the treasure hunt was confusing to her. She had just done it because he had asked. She expressed to Springstead, more than once, how ridiculous the FBI was to be wasting its resources looking for toys. She knew her husband quite well, she said, and he was no spy.

Anette's tiresome defiance prompted Springstead to share with her a couple of details from the investigation. Having monitored many of Anette's prison visits, Springstead knew that Anette thought Regan was about to travel on business when he was arrested. "Did you know that he told his boss that he was going to Orlando on vacation with the family?" Springstead asked.

Anette stared back in silence. This was news to her.

Springstead also told her that Regan had left his wedding ring in the carburetor of his car before catching the shuttle to the airport that afternoon. "If he was just going on a trip for work," she asked, "why would he have taken his ring off?"

The usual annoyance on Anette's face was gone now. She looked stunned.

They drove to the sites in the letter, where teams of agents were already doing searches. The collectible glasses that Anette had buried at the location next to the barn in Crownsville were discovered when the squad supervisor, Lydia Jechorek, accidentally stepped on them, cracking one of them under her heel. Carr and the others would tease her for weeks afterward. "Way to destroy the evidence, Lydia," they would say to her jokingly. At the other location, agents recovered four *Mad* magazines and a couple more glasses.

Over the course of those few hours, Anette went from defiant to shaken. The sight of FBI agents looking for things that she had buried, the knowledge that Regan had lied to his boss and to her, the fact that he'd taken his ring off: all of it appeared to have left her questioning her previous judgment. By the time Springstead drove her back home, Anette could no longer deny the bizarreness of Regan's request that she bury toys. Perhaps she shouldn't have complied.

In another shakedown of Regan's cell around the same time, jail staff found more documents, some hidden under his mattress. One was a note to a fellow inmate, offering him coffee and cookies and popcorn—along with money—in return for having him mail a handwritten letter to one of his sisters. That letter—which the sister was supposed to send on to Anette—included a map of a park in Farmingdale where he wanted Anette to bury a few sheets of code to be solved for the treasure hunt, together with a letter to his kids introducing them to the hunt. He hadn't succeeded in getting this letter out.

Investigators also learned that Regan had made a trip to the forests of the Pinelands National Reserve in New Jersey in early 2001 to bury a stack of magazines as part of a future treasure hunt he was creating for his children. Standing at that location, he'd filmed a short video of himself giving directions to the kids on how they could find the treasure. Agents had found the videotape at his house and subsequently dug up the buried magazines as well.

Putting all of these pieces together, Carr and his fellow investigators could see what Regan's game plan was. He was literally attempting to plant evidence to support his "treasure hunt" defense, which he'd begun contriving by generating the fake codes and word puzzles in prison shortly after his arrest. From the video he'd shot in the pine forests, it was evident that he'd begun thinking of this alibi well before he was arrested. Now, having learned that the FBI had surveilled him for months and had seen him walk into wooded areas on multiple occasions, he needed more buried objects—besides the magazines—to account for that behavior. Despite having his back to the wall, or perhaps because of it, he believed he could still outsmart the government and cover up his crime.

In a speech at West Point Military Academy in June 2002, President George W. Bush declared that the United States had to be prepared, in certain circumstances, to strike a potential threat before it became a real one. This new defense doctrine of preemption, the administration explained, was necessary to shield the United States and its allies against the possibility of large-scale attacks by terrorist groups and terror-supporting regimes. In Bush's words, "If we wait for threats to fully materialize, we will have waited too long. . . . Our security will require transforming the military you will lead—a military that must be ready to strike at a moment's notice in any dark corner of the world. And our security will require all Americans to be forward-looking and resolute, to be ready for preemptive action when necessary to defend our liberty and to defend our lives."

The American public and the rest of the world didn't need to parse the speech to understand what Bush meant. He was laying the groundwork for a preemptive strike against Iraq. On September 12, 2002, he told the United Nations that unless UN resolutions against the Iraqi regime were enforced, the United States would have no choice but to act unilaterally. A month later, the U.S. Congress gave the president authorization to attack Iraq, and the U.S. military began gearing up for war.

As the stage for this inevitable conflict was being set, the imperative to find what Regan might have stolen continued to gain urgency. In the months after Regan's arrest, the FBI had probed his daily computer logs at the NRO in fine detail to assess the full breadth of classified material he may have taken. Investigators had been able to ascertain, in addition to the grainy picture they had already constructed of his Intelink accesses, when and for how long he had visited the two high-speed copier rooms proximate to his office suite, where employees had to badge in both to collect printouts and to make photocopies. Even by a conservative estimate, the time he'd spent in those rooms over the two years prior to his retirement would have been enough for him to squirrel away thousands of pages of documents—far more than the eight hundred pages he claimed in his offer to the Libyans. To make things worse for the government, agents learned, Regan had served as the keeper of a library of classified training videos at his division. It could be reasonably assumed that he'd copied some of those as well.

Unable to decipher the three cryptic "letters" Regan was carrying in his blue folder at the time of his arrest, the FBI pursued other avenues to determine where he might have hidden the stolen materials. The searches of the woods by the highway in Farmingdale, the area behind the handball courts at Farmingdale High School, and the parks in Bowie had all been unfruitful, but there was no question of giving up. Investigators downloaded the waypoints stored on Regan's GPS to derive locations that he might have driven to before he was put under constant surveillance. They visited cemeteries, a favored site for dead drops. It didn't advance the search.

They thought through the steps Regan had to have taken to hide the materials. Before burying documents, the agents reasoned, he would have had to store them somewhere outside the NRO. With four kids running around at home, as well as the paranoia he had exhibited about being surveilled, he would not have kept the documents in his house, at least not for the entire time it took him to execute the conspiracy. A logical place to store them would have been a public storage facility.

Carr and a veteran analyst named Marc Reeser pored over Regan's credit card statements. Sprinkled among the hundreds of charges, many of which were for restaurants, Carr and Reeser found several car-rental payments showing that Regan frequently rented cars for two or three days at a time. They also noticed that although he was prolific in using his credit cards, putting every single expense on them, there was a pattern of short gaps in his spending when no charges on them would appear for a couple of days. What was he doing on those days?

The investigators went to the car-rental companies to dig deeper. It turned out that Regan had rented cars on a few occasions in addition to the instances reflected on his credit card bills. He'd paid for these other rentals in cash. Their timing coincided with the periods when his credit cards were inactive, suggesting that Regan may have been covering his tracks on these trips.

The trips were usually made over a span of two days. From the odometer readings on the rented vehicles, the agents could see that Regan drove anywhere between 200 and 300 miles, suggesting a destination within approximately 150 miles of where he'd started. Carr and Reeser sat down with a map, put pins down at the starting locations—typically in the Washington, D.C., area—and used a string to draw circles with a radius of 100 to 150 miles around the pins. The towns that fell on these circles were candidate locations where Regan could have gone to store or bury classified materials.

Using cell phone records and other information, Carr and Reeser narrowed down the list of areas to focus on. The likeliest location they came up with lay just southeast of Richmond, along I-64 East, which they knew Regan often took to go to Virginia Beach. Investigators checked out several public storage facilities there, but the effort was in vain. They wouldn't realize until later how close they had come.

After the FBI had dug up the things that Anette had buried at Regan's behest, prosecutors indicated to the defense that the government was considering charging Anette with obstruction of justice. Like the notice to seek the death penalty, declaring the intent of prosecuting Anette was a not-so-subtle hint from the government to Regan that pleading guilty was his best legal option. "I can't believe they are going to go after the mother of four children," Regan wrote to Anette when he learned about the possibility. Still, he refused to budge from his stance.

For months, Anette had pleaded with him to reconsider. In one of her letters, she starkly laid out the two choices she felt he had before him: taking a plea deal, which would guarantee that he would return home one day, or rolling the dice and possibly dying in prison. She begged him, for the sake of the family, not to go to trial. It wasn't that Regan was uncaring about the family: his letters to her and the children, sprinkled with misspellings, often reflected deep concern for their well-being. If there's a grease fire on the stove, don't throw water on it; douse it with baking powder, he advised in one. Don't forget to unplug the Christmas tree lights at night or else the house could burn down, he cautioned. He exhorted the kids to work hard at school, reminding them that he wanted them to grow up to be doctors or engineers or scientists. The kids shared with him what they'd been for Halloween and asked when he was going to be back with them. The youngest child—who had turned three—sent him a drawing of a flower with the words "I love you" scrawled next to it in black marker.

Despite those heartbreaking exchanges, Regan was unyielding to Anette's entreaties and to his lawyers' attempts to persuade him. He told Anette that he was convinced he didn't have long enough to live to make a plea deal worth considering. The nagging ache in his stomach, he believed, was the symptom of an as-yet-undiagnosed illness that would kill him within a decade. In any case, he was innocent, he insisted; he would be able to prove it in court. It was as if nothing, not even his family, mattered more to him than his fantasy image of himself as a man smart enough to outmaneuver the world.

On December 26, 2002, with just over a month to go before Regan's trial, the defense filed in court a motion asking for the trial to be postponed. It wasn't that his lawyers wanted more time to prepare. They were worried that Regan wouldn't get a fair trial because of events unfolding thousands of miles away in the Middle East.

Days earlier, George W. Bush had ordered a deployment of U.S. troops to the Persian Gulf in a buildup expected to culminate in war. Although UN inspectors were on the ground in Iraq looking for weapons of mass destruction, U.S. officials were skeptical that the inspections would be able to uncover WMDs that Saddam Hussein was intent on hiding. The only way to get the Iraqi regime to be transparent, Bush and his advisers believed, was through military force.

The defense argued that by January 27—when the trial was scheduled to begin—the United States was expected to urge the United Nations to authorize an offensive against Iraq, after which U.S. troops deployed in the region would proceed to launch an invasion. "There is every likelihood that American lives will be lost," the motion read. "This will happen just as the jury is considering Mr. Regan's innocence or guilt, and deciding if he will live or die." Under those circumstances, Regan's lawyers submitted, the jurors would find it difficult not to feel prejudiced against a defendant charged with trying to sell defense secrets to the very nation that the United States was at war with. "We ask that the court consider putting off this trial until the current situation is resolved," the motion read.

The government wasn't amenable to the delay. The trial had originally been scheduled for June 2002, the prosecution pointed out, and had been pushed back to January 2003 only at the request of the defense. And since the United States had been engaged in conflict with Iraq for a decade, the prosecution argued, the imminence of a full-scale war didn't change the circumstances enough to warrant a postponement.

The defense may have had more luck anywhere other than the Eastern District of Virginia, which had a reputation as one of the fastest federal courts in the country. It was—and continues to be—referred to as a "rocket docket." The judge, Gerald Bruce Lee, was of the mind that postponing the trial an indefinite period— possibly years—would not be fair to the government or to Regan. He sided with the prosecution.

Before the trial could begin, Judge Lee had to lay down special rules for the hearings to allow the use of classified evidence in the courtroom. They flowed from a law called the Classified Information Procedures Act (CIPA), which was enacted in 1980 to resolve an old dilemma faced by the executive and the judiciary. Over the prior decades, especially through the seventies, the government became increasingly wary of what came to be known as "graymail"—actions taken by a defendant in a criminal case to reveal or threaten to reveal classified information in the course of a trial. Since the government couldn't know in advance if the defendant would end up disclosing or compelling the disclosure of defense-related secrets in open court, the government was often forced to forgo prosecution for fear of the potential damage to national security. The government also had to shy away from prosecuting crimes relating to national security where the government would have to unveil classified information to secure a conviction. This bind was a serious vulnerability for the government because it offered a sort of default immunity to traitors lurking within the intelligence community.

CIPA was enacted to close the loophole and balance the need for protecting national secrets with the defendant's right to a fair trial. Under the law, both the defense and the prosecution are required to notify the court in advance if they plan to introduce any classified information, in which case the court must make arrangements to safeguard it.

Those arrangements were in place at the federal courthouse in Alexandria on the morning of January 27, 2003, when U.S. marshals escorted Regan, dressed in an orange jumpsuit, into a high-ceilinged courtroom for the opening of the trial. His parents, Anne and Michael, had driven down from Farmingdale with Regan's sisters to attend. They were shocked at how much weight he had lost in prison. He gave them a wan smile.

The twelve jurors who would decide his fate—among them a newly naturalized U.S. citizen originally from Poland—took their seats, facing a television monitor on which they could view any classified evidence that was to be presented. The evidence was also visible on separate monitors situated in front of the judge, the witness, the prosecution, and the defense. All of the screens were turned away from the gallery so that nobody else in the courtroom could see the evidence. The jury was also given copies of some classified documents. Judge Lee explained how witnesses for the defense and the prosecution would testify regarding any classified evidence presented, using what's known as a silent-witness rule.

"Under this rule, the witnesses will answer questions posed by the lawyers referring you to portions of the documents projected on the screen," he said. "The witness may answer using generic terms like 'nation' or 'country,' 'technique' or 'location,' and then identify the specific nation, location or technique at issue by pointing you to a written document projected on your screen. In this way, the witness can answer without revealing classified information in open court." And with that began the trial of Brian Patrick Regan, the first individual in American history to face the death penalty for attempted espionage.

The American justice system holds prosecutors to a high standard. It's not enough that they prove that the defendant committed the alleged crime. They must prove it to the jury "beyond a reasonable doubt." That phrase, oft heard in American courtrooms, has important implications for the defendant's approach to winning an acquittal. All the defense needs to be able to do is inject doubt into the minds of jurors about the prosecution's claims.

That's what Regan's lawyers set about doing as the government laid out its evidence against the former Air Force master sergeant, one key element being the encoded geocoordinates of the Iraqi and Chinese missile sites that Regan had on him when he was arrested. The prosecution alleged that Regan intended to share these coordinates with Iraqi and Chinese embassy officials to establish his bona fides and prove that he had access. The sites' coordinates and the dates they were imaged, prosecutors argued, would have helped Iraq and China know what targets the United States was watching and when, which in turn would have helped the two countries improve their methods of concealing similar sites in the future.

The defense claimed the information wouldn't have been remotely useful to Iraq, China, or any rival intelligence service. "What Mr. Regan had with him at Dulles Airport on August 23 was worthless," Jonathan Shapiro, one of his lawyers, said in the defense's opening argument. "It wasn't even classified. It had no value to a foreign nation." Even if Regan had shared those coordinates with Iraq or with China, the defense claimed, no harm would have come to the United States.

At the core of the argument was the question of what the government could legitimately claim as a secret worth protecting. The Department of Defense and other U.S. agencies spend considerable time and effort determining the classification level for various kinds of information collected by the government. The definitions of these different tiers of sensitivity sound simple enough. Information that would cause "serious damage" to national security if made public is labeled "Secret." The stamp "Top Secret" is used to classify information whose public disclosure would cause "exceptionally grave damage" to national security.

Those pithy definitions, however, mask a byzantine and often subjective process by which classification officials decide what level of secrecy to ascribe to a document. To most outsiders, this labeling can seem like a pointless exercise in bureaucracy, but within the government, those labels guide who within the intelligence community can access a certain piece of information and how the information needs to be handled.

Investigators hadn't found any documents stamped "Secret" or "Top Secret" among Regan's possessions, which the defense saw as an opening for casting doubt on the claim that he was planning to transmit secrets to Iraq and China. The two satellite images that Regan had looked at on Intelink on the day of his arrest may have been classified, but the information that he had derived from them didn't qualify as a secret, his lawyers argued.

To support that contention, the defense brought in Maynard Anderson, a former Pentagon official, as an expert witness. Anderson, whose job included giving the Department of Defense policy advice on keeping classified information secure, testified that the United States' photography of military sites using spy satellites was well-known to other nations. "And on the basis of that kind of knowledge, in my opinion, it would not be a surprise to an Iraqi official—intelligence official or otherwise—to learn that we were able to identify the location of a mobile missile site at a particular time on a particular day," he said.

The prosecution sought to dispel any ambiguity the jurors might have felt about the value of the coordinates by laying out precisely what the Iraqis and the Chinese would have gained from the information. A key witness the government relied on for this purpose was Lieutenant General David Deptula, who had served as the principal planner of U.S. Air Force strikes during the First Gulf War and later commanded operations to enforce the northern no-fly zone. During both those stints, he had experienced Iraqi air defense tactics firsthand while flying F-15s over the country.

Iraqi forces were known to lay what the Americans called a SAMbush, which involved luring the enemy's planes into a zone where they could be surprised by surface-to-air missiles fired from launchers concealed somewhere on the terrain. During the First

Gulf War, the tactic helped Saddam's men down a few dozen air-craft belonging to coalition forces. During the enforcement of the no-fly zones a few years later, the Iraqis found SAMbushes increasingly difficult to pull off because of the United States' ability to use satellite imagery to detect where mobile missile launchers, including SA-3s, were being moved.

If Regan had handed over to the Iraqis the coordinates of one of their missile sites and the date it was imaged, it could have helped them to make their SAMbushes more effective, Deptula told the jury. "The potential exists for them to deceive us by allowing us to think that that missile system is still there when, in fact, just prior to our arrival in the vicinity, they might move the system to a different location, thinking that we would still believe it's where it was in its original location, thereby surprising us," he said.

As it happened, the Iraqis had moved that SA-3 to a new site not long after the image Regan reviewed on Intelink had been photographed. The United States located the system in subsequent satellite images and destroyed it in an air strike on August 27, 2001.

The ability of that particular SA-3 to inflict harm on American pilots wouldn't be the only concern if Regan had shared the coordinates with the Iraqis. It would have helped the adversary in the longer term, Deptula explained. "Just by virtue of the fact that the information was available to the Iraqis that we knew the type of weapon system indicates to them that their practice of concealment and deception of the weapon system was not effective, which would therefore cause them to react in a number of different ways," he said. "And that's perhaps recognizing that their concealment techniques are not working and they could take measures to then conceal the systems to a greater degree than they currently have." The future impact on American pilots could be deadly.

The smoking gun the prosecution presented to the jury was the letters found on Regan's laptop. To establish criminal intent, the government couldn't have asked for a starker and more unambiguous exhibit than the portion of the letter that read: "I am willing to commit espionage against the United States by providing your country with highly classified information." It was a line that the jury heard numerous times over the course of the trial, including when Carr read out the letter, word for word, in his testimony.

The defense's tack was to question the validity of the letters as evidence. Why had it taken the FBI so long to find them? Regan's lawyers asked. After all, investigators had seized the Gateway on the same evening that Regan was arrested; the bureau's digital forensics experts had searched the hard drive right away. "Nothing was found for six months when suddenly this letter materialized," Jonathan Shapiro pointed out in the defense's opening argument. He didn't allege any impropriety explicitly, but the implication of those remarks couldn't have been lost on the jury. At worst, the government had planted the letters on the computer. At best, agents had mishandled the laptop's hard drive, which meant that the evidence produced from it wasn't trustworthy.

The prosecution had anticipated this line of questioning and had spent months preparing for it. Shortly after the letters had been discovered, the FBI sought the help of Mark Walker, an engineer at Microsoft, to figure out when Regan had created those documents and how they ended up in the Gateway's slack space. As one of the architects of Microsoft Word, Walker was not just well qualified to assist with this analysis. He had had a specific role in developing Word's autosave feature, which was how the evidence was captured by the hard drive despite Regan's efforts to cover his tracks.

The FBI arranged for a security clearance for Walker, so that he could review a copy of the hard drive, first sitting in a Sensitive Compartmented Information Facility in Seattle, an agent looking over his shoulder, and later at the Washington Field Office with Carr and other investigators. It wasn't hard to deduce that Regan had used a floppy disk while working to type the plaintext and encoded versions of the letters addressed to the different countries. Because of the autosave feature of Word, designed to prevent users from losing their work in the event of a crash, the data was periodically saved into the temporary directory of the computer's hard disk. As a result, multiple versions of the letter—in various stages of editing and completion—were stored in the slack space. Regan deleted these temporary files, but the data remained. At one point, Regan even reformatted his hard disk, perhaps hoping to destroy any residual data, but that didn't help either.

From the different versions and other associated data on the hard disk, Walker and the investigators were also able to deduce that Regan had copied and pasted different portions of his letter numerous times, making minor changes to the text to customize the letter for specific countries. With each copy-and-paste operation, he left a digital trail. Walker wrote a program to extract the time stamps from the headers of the different documents, which showed that Regan had begun drafting the letter in April 2000 and continued working on it for several months, all the way until November. The timeline matched what Carr's team had pieced together from other facts. In Regan's letter, he had helpfully converted for his potential buyers his asking price of $13 million into a figure of 2.24 billion Swiss francs, which worked out to an exchange rate that investigators determined had occurred only twice in recent history: once in 1989 and a second time in April 2000. And the FBI already knew that Regan had mailed his three packages to the Libyan embassy sometime in mid-November 2000, consistent with the computer evidence indicating when he'd made his last changes to the letter.

In the courtroom, of course, the prosecution had to rely on the computer evidence; it wasn't prepared to discuss what had been mailed. Walker took the stand and described how the Gateway had saved the different document versions. Some had been saved under the login name "Government User," some under "Valued Gateway customer" and yet others under "Eric33," which matched an e-mail address Regan used: Eric33@erols.com. There wasn't any doubt that he had authored the letter.

The defense didn't have any technical grounds to challenge Walker's analysis. Instead, Ginsberg sought to convince the jury that none of the letters, barring an incomplete version that Regan had spent little time on, had ever been printed. She asked Walker pointedly if another, more complete version of the letter—entered as evidence—was printed.

"It's possible that it was printed," Walker said. If the document had been loaded onto a floppy disk and printed from a computer other than the Gateway, he explained, there wouldn't be a record of it on the Gateway's hard drive. "The lack of a print date doesn't necessarily mean it wasn't printed, whereas the existence of a print date generally indicates that it was printed."

"So, basically, you are saying almost anything is possible?" Ginsberg asked.

"No, it's just that the implication only works one way," Walker answered. "The existence of the date means it's printed. The non-existence of a date doesn't indicate either way."

Aside from trying to refute the government's evidence, Regan's defense embraced a theme that was decidedly unflattering to him. Their contention was that Regan was too naïve—stupid, even—to really be a spy. Throughout the trial, his lawyers painted him as an eccentric, absentminded character who lacked the intellectual wherewithal to pull off an espionage plot against the mighty U.S. government. At the most, he was acting out a spy fantasy.

After having questioned the validity of the letter found on the Gateway, the defense made fun of it, noting how silly it sounded in tone and content. No honest-to-goodness traitor intending to profit from his country's secrets would have written such a letter, his lawyers argued. "He wants to be anonymous and he says, 'Since I do not want to be caught and you should not want me to be caught, I'll remain anonymous,'" Ginsberg told the jury. "Does a person who is really intending to convince a foreign country that he's a spy say, 'If I'm caught, no other agent will attempt to work for you or for your country for fear of being compromised'?"

The asking price of $13 million was just as ridiculous, she claimed, considering that no spy in American history had made even close to that amount. The complicated instructions in the letter for how the transfer of secrets was to take place, without compromising Regan's anonymity, only underscored his naïveté, Ginsberg said, noting that "the kind of minute detail in this letter is so childlike and so improbable that no serious foreign power would ever believe that this was someone they would risk dealing with." On top of it all were those numerous spelling errors that according to the defense were indicative of thoughtless amateurishness rather than of cunning conspiracy.

Ginsberg also downplayed the materials seized from Regan at the airport. That the government's top cryptanalysts—including NSA mathematicians and Dan Olson—had failed to make sense of the handwritten sheets he was carrying in the manila folder, she argued, suggested that their contents weren't any kind of code at all but gibberish. The Tupperware containers, the glue, the plastic shovel, and the GPS device—all these things in his suitcase that the government had alleged were intended for executing a dead drop—were in the defense's interpretation nothing more than evidence of Regan's idiosyncratic ways.

To dispel the notion of Regan as a harmless pretender, the prosecution laid out evidence of his meticulous planning. This wasn't some dumb guy with an impulsive, half-baked idea; this was somebody who had considered every step he needed to take to bring his plot to fruition. Whatever flaws existed in the plan, and whatever errors he'd made along the way—such as leaving his Internet browser open at the Crofton library, thus allowing agents to see that he'd been looking for embassy addresses—didn't take anything away from the treasonous nature of his conspiracy.

Nor was there any doubt, the prosecution argued, of how committed he was to his scheme, evidenced by all the effort he'd expended in preparation. He had mined Intelink with increasing regularity for months prior to his retirement, which showed that he never thought of turning back. While the defense claimed that he needed to surf Intelink regularly to do his job, the search terms he had used—like "Top Secret Libya" and "Top Secret Iraq"—indicated a more nefarious intent. Carr likened it to a teenager searching the Internet for XXX porn. Later, he had spent weeks drafting his offer letter to different intelligence services, and then spent more than a hundred hours encoding the text, as reflected by the time stamps found on the Gateway.

That wasn't all. In August 2000, as he neared retirement, he had written to a man named John Clark, a privacy consultant in California, requesting information on how to open an offshore account. He was evidently making plans for how to protect the money he was going to make from his treason. In this letter, which he'd written under the name of Louis Goliwas—an individual who used to live at Regan's address in Bowie years earlier—Regan mentioned that he'd learned of Clark from J. J. Luna. Agents discovered that J. J. Luna was a privacy consultant and that Regan had come across Clark's name in a book authored by Luna, *How to Be Invisible*.

When Carr read the book, he found advice in it on how to hide things "in a way that not even Janet Reno nor the ATF" could track down. Specifically, Luna suggests burying the object in a "state-owned desert wilderness" a certain distance away from a landmark there, such as "a distinctive rock," and taking a picture of the landmark, along with a GPS recording of its latitude and longitude. Carr and his fellow investigators speculated that Regan might have followed those instructions in stashing the stolen secrets, though that hadn't helped the FBI find them.

The prosecution coupled Luna's instructions with some of the cryptic notes found in Regan's van—including the one with the words "Turkey-block" and "dirt-log" that also contained apparent geocoordinates—to make the point that Regan had likely buried the "800 pages of classified information" that he had talked about in the letters drafted to Iraq and Libya. On the Gateway, investigators had also found Regan's notes to himself on what, according to the prosecution, were cautionary measures for secreting documents taken from the NRO. "Moving into house to see if anyone is following you. Get ultraviolet stamp marked packages to make sure the seals were not open, store in outside building, switch to van when moving packages. This will throw off any transmitters on my car," the notes read.

These words weren't the aimless self-talk of someone engaging in fantasy, Gillis said in his closing arguments for the prosecution. And there was no reason to think that Regan would not have been taken seriously by countries like Iraq and Libya. "My God, can you imagine what Saddam Hussein would have done with the information that he was offering and with the information that he had access to?" Gillis asked the jury. He emphasized that Regan was fully cognizant of the harm his actions would cause to the United States. Despite what the defense "may want you to think," he said, "the defendant is not stupid."

On February 20, 2003, after several days of deliberation, the jury convicted Regan on two counts of attempted espionage—for Iraq and for China—and one count of gathering national defense information to aid foreign governments. He was acquitted of the charge of attempting to spy for Libya—an irony, given how the FBI's investigation began. Thankfully for Regan and his family, the jury decided against the death penalty on the grounds that he hadn't offered the Iraqis documents directly related to nuclear weapons, military satellites, communications intelligence, or war plans, which under the espionage statutes meant his offense wasn't a capital crime. Sentencing was scheduled for May.

After he was convicted, Regan was put into solitary confinement, which meant having to spend more than twenty-three hours a day locked up inside his cell, with no contact whatsoever with other inmates. His only way of passing the time was by reading books borrowed from the jail library. As was customary, the guards would let him out for half an hour to go take a shower, at a time of day that was convenient to them. Regan already knew that he was likely to get a life sentence. The prospect of serving that term under solitary confinement—which prosecutors had hinted could be necessary to prevent him from divulging secrets to fellow inmates—terrified him.

Meanwhile, the threat of Anette's being prosecuted loomed in the background. During the run-up to his trial, Regan hadn't focused much attention on the possibility that she, too, could end up in prison, but now the thought of it was inescapable. Who would take care of the kids if that happened? Through his lawyers, he reached out to the government to indicate that he was finally willing to cooperate. Not long before, he'd attempted to blackmail the government; now he was having to contend with the government's own strong-arm tactics.

In the days that followed, the prosecution drew up a sentencing agreement with Regan's lawyers. According to the terms, the government would not pursue any charges against Anette for obstruction of justice. Although Regan's retirement benefits would automatically be forfeited, the government would arrange for Anette to receive a part of his military pension. In exchange, Regan would accept a sentence of life in prison, but he would not be kept in solitary confinement. And most important—from the government's point of view—he would help the government recover the classified materials he had hidden.

On the morning of March 20, just hours after the United States began bombing targets in Baghdad to begin the war against Iraq, U.S.

marshals escorted Regan into Judge Lee's courtroom in Alexandria to be sentenced. After reviewing the agreement, the judge looked at Regan, who stood before him wearing a green prison jumpsuit.

"Mr. Regan, are you sure you're willing to take life in prison?"

"Yes, Your Honor." According to the agreement, he was giving up the right to appeal his conviction or his sentence going forward. He said he was agreeing to the deal to "protect my wife and children from any more pain and suffering."

Judge Lee reminded him that a life sentence in the federal system meant no possibility of being granted parole. Regan would never again be a free man.

"I feel a life sentence is excessive in my case," Regan said. "I never harmed anyone. I'm entering into this to protect my family."

If he was expecting any sympathy from the judge, there was none forthcoming.

"You betrayed your country's trust," Judge Lee said. "There's no doubt that your attempted espionage put our nation's intelligence gathering at risk. You have joined the list of infamous spies."

With that, he approved the sentence. For Carr and other FBI agents present in the room, it was a moment of triumph after what had been an arduous two and a half years. Justice had been done. But the task of finding the secrets Regan had stolen still lay ahead.

CHAPTER 9

THE SEARCH
FOR BURIED SECRETS

The morning after the sentencing, Steve Carr signed Regan out of a holding cell at the federal courthouse in Alexandria and escorted him into a conference room. Seated around a table there were about a dozen people, including the prosecuting and defense attorneys, as well as representatives from the CIA, the NSA, and the NRO. Carr took off Regan's handcuffs and asked him to sit down. It was the first time that he'd had a chance to speak to Regan since arresting him eighteen months earlier.

The conversation today was going to be a lot different. To make sure that it got off to a good start, Bob Rice, the NRO counterintelligence agent, had brought along a bottle of Mountain Dew, Regan's favorite drink, which sat on the table in front of Regan, along with some snacks. Regan settled into his chair and looked around the room, his face devoid of expression.

"How are you feeling about your situation?" Carr asked, sitting at the head of the table.

"It stinks that I'll be in jail for the rest of my life," Regan replied.

Carr got down to business. "Brian, we want to hear your story," he said.

Speaking in a flat monotone, Regan described how he'd taken materials out of the NRO and buried them. For Carr, hearing Regan's account of his crime was the equivalent of a scientist finally getting the requisite field data to empirically validate a well-developed theory. Confirming what Carr and Reeser had inferred in the course of the investigation, Regan admitted to having moved the stolen secrets out of the NRO first to his house, and then to a public storage facility. He also admitted that he'd mailed his espionage offer packages to both Iraq and Iran in addition to Libya.

Although there were a million questions that Carr wanted to ask to fill in the details of Regan's plot, he had to stay focused on the task of recovering the secrets. "How do we go about finding the stuff?" he asked.

After eighteen months of attempting to mislead investigators, blackmail the government, and fabricate a defense, Regan had no reason left to be secretive. He revealed that he had buried nineteen packages: twelve of them in Pocahontas State Park in Virginia and another seven in Patapsco Valley State Park in Maryland. He had planned on selling only the packages he'd hidden in Virginia, he said. The secrets he'd stashed in Maryland were more sensitive; he claimed he'd never intended to give those away. He'd hidden them with the notion that he might be able to leverage them to negotiate with the government if he ever got caught.

The sheets with trinomes that he'd had on him at the airport—marked Letter S-I134, Letter M-I134, and Letter A-341I—contained encrypted geocoordinates of the hiding locations in Pocahontas.

Regan explained that each "letter" was meant for a different country. S-I134 contained the coordinates for the sites where he'd hidden packages for Iraq (*S* representing Saddam Hussein); M-I134 contained the coordinates for the secrets he'd assembled for Libya (*M* for Muammar Gaddhafi); and A-341I (*A* being a reference to Ali Khamenei) had the sites with packages for Iran. Regan also explained how he'd tailored the three sets of packages keeping in mind the geopolitical context and intelligence needs of each country. The documents he'd compiled for Iraq, for instance, included satellite images of military facilities in Iran and other countries in the region. Similarly, for Iran, he'd assembled images and reports relating to the Iraqi military and the militaries of other neighboring countries.

He'd decided at the last minute not to include in these sets satellite intelligence about Israel's military, even though he had printed such documents out from Intelink along with everything else. His reasoning was that giving away classified information about Israel—the United States' closest ally in the region—to countries that were sworn enemies of Israel would be directly harmful to the national security of the United States. That's why he'd mulched those documents in the bathtub of the motel in Chester and thrown them into a dumpster.

The people in the room listened with rapt attention as Regan spoke, his dull delivery notwithstanding. He paused every now and then to take a sip of Mountain Dew. The scheme he had used to encrypt the Pocahontas coordinates, he said, was based on an employee phone list from the NRO. He'd had the list with him when he was arrested at the airport, but it hadn't struck investigators as unusual. Regan said he'd buried copies of the list at several locations in Chantilly as well as in Farmingdale; since it was the key to his code, he had been paranoid about misplacing it. That's what he'd been doing when surveillance specialists saw him disappear into the woods behind the handball court at Farmingdale High the weekend before he was arrested.

Some of the notes with cryptic writings that agents had found in Regan's van contained references to these locations. Carr had brought those notes along this morning, and when he laid them out on the table, Regan told him what they meant. "Turkey-block" was a reference to the Talkin Turkey deli near the NRO, where Regan had often gone for lunch—he'd buried a copy of the phone list there. He'd buried another one off the highway by Galyan's sporting goods store in Chantilly; his code for that location included "35steps-dirt-log-Mexico"—a reference to the number of steps he had to walk south of a fallen log to get to the spot.

Carr took notes on how the trinome code worked, but there was no need to decrypt the trinomes to find the Virginia packages, Regan said. He had written down the plaintext coordinates of the Pocahontas sites on a sheet of paper and rolled it up in a toothbrush container that could be found buried next to I-95 sixty miles south of Washington, D.C., at a spot next to Exit 130A. In the container, Regan said, agents would also find, in encrypted form, the coordinates for the seven packages in Maryland. The code he'd used for these was based on his junior high school yearbook.

Carr had sent an agent to buy some food for Regan. The agent returned with a ham and cheese sandwich and placed it before Regan. The U.S. marshals weren't happy, but Carr didn't care. He knew he was going to need Regan's help again soon. For now, his mind was racing to make plans for the recovery operations in Virginia. Shortly after one p.m., after wrapping up the day's interview, he called Lydia Jechorek.

"Lydia," he said. "We're going on a road trip."

The convoy of vehicles sped south along I-95, having set out from the FBI's Washington Field Office bright and early on March 22, a Saturday. Carr was at the wheel of his personal Ford Excursion, a roomy SUV that he typically used on the weekends for transporting band instruments for his kids and taking Boy Scouts on camping trips. This morning, all of the seats in it were occupied by agents from Carr's squad. The back of the vehicle was loaded with shovels and metal detectors and other gear for executing what the agents hoped would be a successful treasure hunt.

Riding in the other cars were officials from the NRO, the CIA, and the NSA—the rightful custodians of much of that treasure. Following the directions that Regan had given the day before, Carr led the convoy down the highway past Fredericksburg before turning around and driving back in the opposite direction, on I-95 North, until he got to the sign for Exit 130A. He pulled his truck over to the shoulder and parked right in front of the exit sign. The other cars pulled up behind him. Everybody got out.

The agents walked uphill from the sign as Regan had directed, inspecting the ground with ground-penetrating radar and a metal rod to probe the soil. Spring was still a few weeks away, and the trees and bushes along the highway looked bare. The area the agents were exploring was next to private property fenced by barbed wire; two little boys playing there peeked out from behind a large tree, curious to see what was going on. The sight of so many people walking along the shoulder of the highway drew the attention of a Virginia state trooper driving by, and he came over to inquire about the activity.

The agents flashed him their badges. "We're looking for some evidence," Carr said. The trooper left them alone.

Minutes later, the agents found the toothbrush holder, buried less than three inches under the ground. The discovery seemed surreal to Carr. On the drive down from Washington, he'd felt both an adrenaline rush as well as a niggling doubt, wondering if Regan might be leading the FBI on a wild-goose chase. Now he had no doubt that the search was on the right track.

"Steve, it's wrapped in packing tape," Kathy Springstead yelled out to Carr above the roar of the highway traffic rushing past. "Do you want me to take the tape off?"

If this had been ordinary evidence found in the course of an investigation, it would have had to be handled with the utmost care. The agents would have had to take it into a lab, where forensic examiners would have fingerprinted it and conducted other analysis to link the package to the subject of the investigation. But this wasn't ordinary evidence. Regan's legal fate had already been sealed. There was no need to waste time.

Carr asked Springstead to unwrap the container. "We have to see what's in it," he said.

After cutting through the tape, she peeled off the layers. What lay inside was only the bottom half of the holder—a translucent purple tube with sheets rolled up in it. Since the roll was a couple of inches longer than a toothbrush and wouldn't have fit under the lid of the holder, Regan had left it off. He'd buried the lid—with an identical set of papers—off an exit on the other side of the highway.

The agents unrolled the pages, holding them down against brown paper bags while somebody took digital photographs. Among them was a copy of Regan's encrypted offer letter, his codebook, and the instructions for decryption—the same set of materials he'd mailed to the Libyan embassy. One of the sheets contained some twelve lines of numbers mixed in with letters, which Carr identified as the code for the Maryland coordinates that Regan had talked about. And then there was the information that the agents wanted to act upon immediately: the page on which Regan had put down the plaintext coordinates for the packages buried in Pocahontas.

Besides the other half of the toothbrush holder hidden on the southbound side of I-95, the investigators also dug up a saltshaker that Regan had told them about. It contained the keys to the storage unit Regan had rented near Pocahontas. During the investigation, Carr would have given anything to be able to track down those keys—they would have been a priceless aid in the effort to reconstruct Regan's crime.

At this juncture, however, all he wanted to do was get to Pocahontas State Park as quickly as possible. By two p.m., the convoy was back on the highway, headed eighty miles farther south.

The morning dew was still fresh at Pocahontas on Sunday, March 23, when Carr and his fellow agents began walking through the woods to locate the first of the twelve sites. Bill Lace and Marc Reeser had GPS units with them to guide the way. Geocoordinates can be written in different ways; Regan had followed the "degrees decimal minutes" format. What he had written on the sheet in the toothbrush holder were the three digits after the decimal point for each latitude and longitude. Since the digits that came before the decimal point—the degrees and the minutes—were the same for practically the entire park, he hadn't bothered to write them down. It was simple enough for Lace and Reeser to complete each set of coordinates and plug them into their GPS devices.

They navigated through the tall pines, stepping over fallen logs and broken tree limbs—the apparent wreckage left behind by a storm just days earlier. Some of the agents carried shovels. Others held metal detectors to look for the roofing nails that Regan had said he'd hammered into a tree near every site. Even though the coordinates were sufficient to pinpoint the sites, the nails, Regan had explained, were a backup to help confirm each location, along the lines of what he'd read in J. J. Luna's book. The choice of a state park to bury the materials was itself based on Luna's advice: Regan wanted to pick a place that would be protected from any construction activity in the foreseeable future.

After about fifteen minutes of walking, the agents got to the first site—a flat clearing in the middle of the trees. On a tree about eight feet away, just as Regan had said, they found three nails, hammered into the trunk at approximately chest height. One of the agents began digging at the spot the GPS had pointed to.

After just a few strikes, his shovel hit something soft. He removed the loose dirt to uncover the top of a package, wrapped in a garbage bag. It lay barely a foot under the ground.

"We found one!" more than one person yelled out to the others. Somebody gave Carr a high five. His face was flushed with excitement.

The dozen or so people in the group gathered around the site for a photo, with the package still in the ground. Afterward, the agents hauled it out. Somebody laid a tarp on the ground nearby. Springstead slit open the package with a knife and laid out some of the documents on the tarp. As the agents had expected, the pages were printouts of satellite images and intelligence reports, most of them stamped "Top Secret." Information that—according to Regan—"could start a war."

Over the next hour and a half, excited shouts of "Found another one!" rang out in the forest time and again as the agents went from one site to the next. In scanning the trees with the metal detectors while searching for the nails, the agents ran into a problem: it was hard to remember which trees they had already scanned. The solution they came up with was to nick the trunks of the scanned trees with their shovels—a violation that would no doubt have earned them hundreds of dollars in fines, had a park ranger been on the scene. But the excitement in the air was too high for anybody to care. By lunchtime, Carr's team had dug up another five packages from the general area, which along with the first package made up the entire cluster of six that Regan had buried on this side of the park.

The team drove to another part of the park to search for the other six packages. Here, too, they struck gold right away. It was evident that Regan hadn't surveyed this location with much care; he seemed to have been unaware of how high the water table was at some of the spots he had chosen. Digging at one such site in the cluster, agents hauled out a package that was soaking wet.

"Oh God, look at this," the digger said. "Look, he punched a hole in this package."

As Regan would describe in later interviews to Carr, he'd jabbed his pen into that package while burying it to release the air trapped inside. The air had caused parts of the wrapping to puff up. What Regan hadn't noticed was how wet the earth around the hole was. In the two years since, water had spilled onto the documents inside. When Carr and the others inspected them, they saw that worms had buried holes through many of the pages.

Near another site, the agents spotted a piece of plastic stuck on a tree. When they dug up the package at that site, they could see that the plastic had come from the garbage bag that the package was wrapped in. Working in the darkness of night, Regan had evidently failed to notice when the wrapping got caught on the end of a low-hanging tree branch.

By late afternoon, the group had dug up eleven stacks of documents: some of them stuffed in Rubbermaid containers, some held in cardboard boxes, and a few wrapped directly in trash bags. A lot of the materials recovered from the second cluster were soaking wet, the print smudged off here and there. There was just one package left to be recovered.

But Carr's team was having no luck finding it. Lace and Reeser checked and rechecked the coordinates for the site, which resolved to a spot about three hundred yards from the vicinity where the other five packages of this cluster had been found. "Something doesn't seem right," Reeser told Carr. Why would Regan have walked so far away from the other sites to bury this package?

It was past four p.m., and daylight was fast fading in the forest. The group was too exhausted to keep looking. Carr decided it was time to wind up the search for the day. The recovered packages were hauled into the back of the Excursion. They stacked up all the way to the ceiling, blocking the rearview mirror as Carr drove out of Pocahontas before eventually heading back to the Washington Field Office.

When the agents got back to the office, they loaded the packages on dollies and carted them up on the elevator to the floor of the counterintelligence squad. Carr was worried that the thousands of soaked pages among the documents would get mildewed unless they were dried. So he and the others laid out the stacks inside a conference room. Carr went around the office, grabbing every table fan he could find on the cubicle desks. He placed them around the documents and switched them on, turning the room into a make-shift drying chamber. Before he and the others left, they changed the room's passcode so that nobody unrelated to the case would be able to get in.

When Carr pulled into his driveway, it was close to midnight. Despite the day's rich haul, the failure to locate the twelfth package bothered him. Regan had clearly made an error in writing that site's coordinates on the sheet hidden in the toothbrush holder. According to what he'd told Carr, however, he hadn't referred to this sheet when converting the plaintext coordinates into code. He had consulted another piece of paper, which he'd originally re-corded the coordinates on and subsequently destroyed. Assuming that this original sheet didn't contain the same error that had foiled the search for the twelfth package, there was a way to find its correct location, Carr reasoned: by decrypting the trinomes.

Dan Olson had never been able to put the trinomes out of his head. Long after he stopped actively trying to decode them in the late spring of 2002, he had found his mind returning time and again to the knotty problem that those four sheets represented. There was an undeniable sense of frustration associated with the memory. Although his analysis of the trinomes had definitely helped the investigation—his testimony had enabled prosecutors to argue that the trinomes were a code, not a meaningless sequence of numbers—Olson wished he'd succeeded in making a more substantive contribution.

That's why he felt a rush of adrenaline when Carr called him with a request to revisit the code. Carr filled him in on the search: how eleven packages had been found using the plaintext coordinates. Olson's help was needed to find the twelfth package, Carr explained. For Olson, the chance to decrypt the trinomes—even though it wasn't the same thing as cracking them—was a welcome opportunity for closure.

The morning after Carr had returned from Pocahontas, Olson went over to the Washington Field Office. During the debriefing with Regan, Carr had taken notes on how Regan had gone about encrypting the coordinates. He gave them to Olson. Regan's step-by-step directions were so confusing that making sense of them was itself a bit like solving a puzzle. When Olson was finally clear about the scheme, he found an unattended cubicle to sit down in and work on the decryption.

Regan had used two layers of encryption. To convert the coded message into plaintext, he first had to convert each trinome into a two-digit number by following a couple of simple steps. In the first step, the first digit of the trinome had to be "inverted" by using the following table.

```
1 2 3 4 5 6 7 8 9 0
0 9 8 7 6 5 4 3 2 1
```

The digit to be converted had to be looked up in the top row. It would convert to the corresponding digit in the bottom row. If the first digit of the trinome was 1, it would change to the digit right below 1 in the bottom row: 0. If the first digit was 6, the corresponding digit would be 5, and so on.

To convert the second and third digits of the trinome into a single digit, he had to look them up on another table. More on that in a minute, but first the table:

	1	2
1	1	2
2	3	4
3	5	6
4	7	8
5	9	0

The second digit had to be looked up in the leftmost column. It made sense that this column ran from 1 to 5: as Olson had noticed in his early analysis of the trinomes, the second digit in them was never 0 and never greater than 5. Similarly, the third digit of the trinomes was always either 1 or 2. So if the last two digits of a trinome were, say, 41—the single digit it would convert to could be found in the cell where the row corresponding to 4 intersects with the column under 1. That digit, as you can see from the conversion table, is 7.

As an example of the entire conversion from three-digit number to two-digit number, let's consider the first of the 292 trinomes in the message that Regan marked as Letter M-I134. That trinome is 132. Following the rule laid out for conversion of the first digit, 1 becomes 0 (as per the first table). The second and third digits, 32, converted using the second table, become 6. So the trinome 132 is now reduced to 06.

Olson stripped off this first layer of encryption and converted the multiple lines of trinomes representing the three "letters" into a series of two-digit numbers. The second layer of encryption involved the three NRO phone lists that Regan said were his key. Both Olson and the code breakers at the NSA had suspected that Regan might have used a book code of some kind. Olson was pleased to learn that at least this conjecture had been valid. In Regan's scheme, the phone lists essentially served the same purpose as a book.

Using the phone lists, every pair of numbers in the two-digit series derived from the trinomes could be converted into a letter or a digit. (This explained another feature of the letters that Olson had noted earlier: the fact that each constituted an even number of trinomes.) The first two-digit number indicated how many names down on the list you had to go: if the number was 12, say, you had to go down to the twelfth name. The second two-digit number gave the position of the character from that particular listing that the pair represented.

Letter M-I134 began with the following trinomes:

132 111 132 011 012 112 021 142 042 132 042
011 752 121 . . .

Stripping the first layer of encryption translated these to:

06 01 06 11 12 02 13 08 15 08 18 06 18 11 . . .

Each pair in this series stood for a letter or a digit. Demarcating those pairs from one another made the series look something like this:

(06 01) (06 11) (12 02) (13 08) (15 08) (18 06) (18 11) . . .

Now, to decode the first pair of numbers (06 01), the reader of the message had to go down to the sixth name on the particular phone list that was meant to be used as the key. That name happened to be "Saxby, Robert." The first character in the listing was S—and so the pair (06 01) became S.

Converting the rest of the series resolved the opening of the message to: "S T A R T L Y," which was Regan's way of denoting that the coordinates to follow were for a package intended for Libya. Then came the coordinates themselves, encrypted in their entirety: N3720253 and W7734312. (Since each listing contained a name as well as a phone number, Regan could use the list to encrypt both letters and digits.) Read in the "degrees decimal minutes" format, the coordinates represented a latitude of 37 degrees 20.253 minutes and a longitude of 77 degrees 34.312 minutes. Going beyond the coordinates, the message read "FT 7," marking the number of feet to the tree on which the nails had been hammered. This was followed by the word "END." The words "START" and "END" were like bookends—linguistic markers bracketing each set of coordinates.

Olson would eventually decrypt all three letters in this way. But when he came in to work on the trinomes to help find the twelfth package, Carr and his fellow agents still had not gotten ahold of the three phone lists. Despite that handicap, Olson believed he could figure out the desired coordinates.

The reason was that Regan had built into his scheme what cryptanalysts call a "back door"—a way to recover the information in case he lost the key. As with numerous elements of his plot, here, too, he'd thought of a plan B.

His safeguard was to tuck the operative part of the coordinates into the trinomes in a form that could be recovered even without access to the phone lists. Specifically, he had embedded the last four digits of the latitude, the last three digits of the longitude, and the number of feet within the series of two-digit numbers derived from the trinomes. In other words, he'd put these digits only through the first layer of encryption, applying the two tables. He hadn't enciphered them further using the phone lists.

The tricky thing about this "back door" was that there was no obvious marker indicating where in the message it was. Regan had embedded the information as a footnote, immediately following the word that signaled the bookending of one set of coordinates ("END" in the above example). But the only way to find it was to decrypt the entire message, and that required access to the phone lists. It was a catch-22 that defeated the purpose of a back door.

However, Olson had the advantage of knowing eleven of the twelve coordinates, which helped him figure out what the back-door digits for those sites were supposed to be in Regan's scheme. Scanning the two-digit numbers he'd derived from the trinomes, he was able to find those embedded coordinates. That allowed him to make a reasoned guess about where the twelfth set of coordinates, in its abbreviated back-door form, was most likely to be found among the lines and lines of two-digit numbers. He could now focus his attention on a small subset of numbers in the series.

As he studied them, he came across two consecutive pairs of numbers that looked different from the rest.

(02 53) (31 27)

What was odd about the two was that the second number in each pair—53 and 27—was a lot higher than the second number in most other pairs of the series. To convert the first pair into a letter or digit according to Regan's decipherment rules, Olson would have had to find the fifty-third character in the second listing on one of the phone lists. It was unlikely for a name, followed by an extension number, to contain such a large number of characters, Olson thought. The same was true of the second pair. And so, even though Olson didn't have the phone lists, he deduced that the two pairs were not part of the code.

This meant that the numbers written in one string, "02533127," had to be one of Regan's back doors. Olson broke that down into a latitude, longitude, and number of feet and gave it to Carr.

Carr had asked an agent from the squad to stay back near Pocahontas to continue the search for the remaining package. He called him and relayed the coordinates that Olson had derived. Hours later, the agent called him back, exultant. The twelfth trove of secrets had been found.

Having confirmed the right location for the last package, Carr and his fellow investigators realized what Regan had gotten wrong when he wrote down the plaintext coordinates for that site. He had transposed a couple of digits. Once again, as with the spelling errors in his offer letter, his dyslexia was to blame.

With the Virginia packages safely back in the government's custody, Carr turned his attention to the secrets buried in Maryland. Given the relative ease with which the FBI had found the stashes in Pocahontas, Carr was optimistic about recovering the seven packages at Patapsco Valley State Park in short order. He anticipated few challenges in decoding the encrypted coordinates for those sites— with Regan's help—and then digging up the packages.

He couldn't have been more wrong.

CHAPTER 10

MR. EIGHTY PERCENT

One afternoon in early April, Carr rang the doorbell of Anette Regan's house in Bowie. He had called earlier to say that he'd be stopping by with yet another search warrant.

"What are you looking for now?" she had asked on the phone, sounding exasperated. She had expected Regan's sentencing to mark the end of her nightmare. After eighteen months of trauma, she was desperate to piece the shambles of her life back together and find a way forward for herself and the kids. She would have given anything not to have another FBI agent walk through her house ever again.

Carr hadn't told her what the search was for. She answered the door, an irritated look on her face.

"Would you like to see the search warrant?" Carr asked.

"No," she replied.

"OK," he said. "This will take a second."

Stepping into the house, he walked to the bookshelves in one corner of the living room. Regan had told him exactly where to look for what he wanted. Carr bent down to access the bottom bookshelf. Four books in—just as Regan had said—was Regan's junior high school yearbook.

Carr pulled it out and inspected it. The green hardbound cover said "1977" in a large white font, with the words "Mill Lane Junior High" printed across.

Anette watched him from where she stood in the living room. She looked mystified. "What do you want that for?" she asked.

Carr didn't answer the question. Instead he filled out an inventory sheet indicating what he was taking, gave her a copy, and said a polite "Thanks" on his way out.

A day or so later, Carr went back to visit Regan. At the first debriefing session, Regan had not had any difficulty explaining the scheme he had used for the Virginia code. At the time, Carr had not asked him about the Maryland code because the encoded coordinates were yet to be recovered from the toothbrush holder. Now, having obtained both the code sheet and the yearbook on which the code was based, Carr asked Regan to break out the Maryland coordinates.

Regan looked intently at the sheet and went through the yearbook. Finally, after having scrutinized the materials for several minutes, he looked up at Carr apologetically.

He could not remember the key to his own code.

In his six years as a cryptanalyst at the FBI, Olson had collaborated with colleagues of many different backgrounds to break codes. Besides working with fellow cryptanalysts, he had brainstormed with field agents of the bureau, worked with jail authorities, and partnered with linguists when cracking codes written in foreign languages. What he'd never done—or thought he would never do—was work on decrypting a code in collaboration with the person who had written it.

Yet that was the task that Olson had before him when he drove up from Quantico to the Alexandria courthouse one morning in mid-April. Carr was waiting for him. The two men went down to the conference room in the basement where Carr had interviewed Regan before.

In the days prior, Olson had familiarized himself with the code. He didn't have to look closely to see how different it was from the trinomes Regan had used to encrypt the coordinates for the sites in Virginia. The text was typewritten, unlike the Virginia "letters," which had all been written by hand. Even though much of the code did consist of trinomes, these trinomes followed neither of the two rules obeyed by the handwritten trinomes—that of the second digit always being a number from 1 to 5, and the last digit always being 1 or 2. It was hard to find any obvious pattern in them. The series began:

146 051 400 356 370 035 739 190 454 413 . . .

Another thing that was different about the Maryland code was that the trinomes were interspersed with alphanumerical groupings containing three characters—each a two-digit number followed by an *A*. For example, if we pick up the series from where we left off above, at "413" and continuing on to the end of the first line, the text read:

. . . 413 958 431 **13A 11A 40A** 775.

At the top of the sheet, above the twelve lines of code, was an intriguing phrase—the only intelligible text on the sheet. It said: "Number One."

Olson had also spent several hours studying the yearbook, whose pages were filled with mug shots of ninth graders who—along with Regan—had graduated from Mill Lane in 1977. The code had to be based on the pictures and names of the students. Sitting at his desk in Quantico, Olson had tried, unsuccessfully, to uncover the encryption scheme that tied the yearbook to the code sheet.

The U.S. marshals brought Regan into the room and unshackled him. He sat down at the table and nodded a greeting at Carr.

Carr introduced Olson, who was sitting across from Regan.

Regan said he remembered him from the trial, when Olson had taken the stand to testify. "Did you agree with what I said?" Olson asked jokingly. Regan didn't react.

It was the first time that Olson was getting a close look at the man whose trinomes had given him sleepless nights. This morning, however, Olson the code breaker and Regan the code maker were no longer adversaries. In the game of hide-and-seek they had been playing since August 2001, Regan was now as much of a seeker as Olson. Their shared goal was to decipher the encrypted coordinates with the help of the yearbook. Olson's job was to help Regan recall how the code worked.

He slid the yearbook across the table to Regan.

Regan flipped the pages, scanning the rows upon rows of classmates staring back at him, their midteen portraits reminiscent of that twilight zone between childish innocence and youthful, self-confident immaturity. In the rows he spotted the gang from his neighborhood—Brian Wagner, Bob Florio, Cliff Wagner—and friends like Peter Klopfer, who had been with Regan in remedial classes prescribed to slow learners and weathered some of the same insults as Regan. On the twenty-fifth page, at the bottom corner, was Regan himself, looking at the camera with a shy smile, a thick and shiny mop of hair covering his forehead all the way to the tops of his eyebrows.

If these pictures brought back memories of ninth grade, the notes that his classmates had written on the pages brought them into sharper focus. There was the one signed by Richard DiBernardo, thanking Regan for helping him carve a wooden eagle in their shop class. There were others that were far less kind—little reminders of the bruises that Regan's psyche had endured during those adolescent years. "Good luck in 10th grade . . . you'll need it," said one.

Regan also had in front of him a copy of the code sheet.

"Let's start right here at the top," Olson said, pointing to the first line of text on the page. "What is 'Number One'?"

Regan remembered that it was a reference to his own picture. He was Number One.

Olson told Regan what his best guess was for how the trinomes in the code related to the yearbook. He believed the first two digits of each trinome as well as the alphanumeric groups were linked to a picture. Was that a correct assumption? he asked Regan.

Regan confirmed that it was.

Next, Olson drew Regan's attention to an alphanumeric group that occurred seven times through the twelve lines of code. It was 13A. Since Regan had buried seven packages, it appeared to be some kind of marker related to every package. What could it be?

Looking in the yearbook, Olson put his finger on Regan's portrait—Number One—and counted forward to the thirteenth picture. Unlike the other mug shots, this one was a portrait of a student wearing a mask of an old man with a white Amish-style beard and bushy eye-brows. The name printed below it read "Mystery Man."

In the white space between the bottom edge of the picture and the printed name, Regan had written "Frank."

Olson had noticed it earlier while studying the yearbook. All the other handwriting in the book, including comments written by Regan, was in blue ink. "Frank" was the only word scribbled in black, with what Olson was certain was a gel pen. Gel pens didn't really come to market until the 1980s, indicating that Regan couldn't have written that word when he graduated from Mill Lane. Besides, the true identity of the student who had posed as Mystery Man was revealed elsewhere in the yearbook: it wasn't a boy but a girl named Karen.

All of that left no doubt that Regan had labeled Mystery Man as "Frank" when he made the cipher.

What was unique about "Frank" that Regan had needed the name for the encryption? It couldn't have been the number of letters, Olson reasoned, because there were several other names in the yearbook with five letters.

If the first two digits of every trinome represented a picture, Regan could have used a maximum of ninety-nine pictures, count-ing forward from himself. When Olson sorted those ninety-nine names alphabetically by first initial, typing them into an Excel sheet, he saw that none of them began with an *F*.

Right away, it became clear why Regan had thought to write "Frank." He needed an *F*—for "feet."

With that little breakthrough, Regan remembered that all the alphanumeric groups in the code encoded letters and not numbers. Just as 13A resolved to *F* from "Frank," 11A resolved to the first initial of the student whose picture was eleventh from Regan's, and so on. When Olson translated them into letters, the majority of them were revealed to be package descriptions: CD for "Compact Discs," SP for "Small Package," BP for "Big Package," and LP for "Large Package." The letter *T* was interspersed throughout the message as well, representing "tree."

The decoding of the alphabetic characters in the message confirmed that the first two digits of every trinome did indeed signify the position of portraits in the book relative to Regan. It also indicated that the remainder of the text encoded digits. Excited to be on the right track, Olson quizzed Regan about the next step in the decryption. What was the relevant information to be extracted from the picture that a trinome led to? Was it the total number of letters in the name? How was this information supposed to be combined with the trinome's third digit?

Usually one to speak in rapid-fire sentences, Olson had to remind himself to ask the questions slowly and deliberately, as Carr had advised. "Don't overwhelm him," Carr had said, having noticed in prior debriefings that Regan took longer than most people to process and react to what he heard. Olson could now see what Carr meant. Through the afternoon, as he continued to probe Regan, Olson kept hitting a wall. Regan scratched his head and tried out different things with the names in an effort to remember how to move past the pictures. He couldn't.

It was when the discussion had completely stalled that Olson shifted his attention to something he'd noticed earlier but not paid much attention to. It was the series of trinomes in the last two lines of the message—the ones following the last alphanumeric group to appear in the text:

... 833 698 707 231 069 **16A** *141 249 453 062 141 462
454 414 205 629 524 834 205 173 524 219 181 602 472
025 181 496 471 955*

What was surprising about these trinomes (italicized above) was that there were several repeats among them. The numbers 141, 205, and 181 each occurred twice, and the repeats occurred at the same intervals. This was in stark contrast with the trinomes that came before 16A, which were all unique.

In fact, from an analysis of the first two digits of the earlier trinomes, Olson could see that Regan had attempted not to use any picture twice, barring a few exceptions. It was easy to guess why Regan would have taken such care to avoid repetitions: by ensuring that there was no discernible pattern to be discovered in the numbers, he was no doubt striving to make the code harder to break. Why had he abandoned this caution toward the end of the message?

When he'd noticed that anomaly for the first time at Quantico, Olson had chosen to disregard it. It's not unusual for coded messages to contain some garbage or useless information that has been included simply to add noise. Olson had assumed that the trinomes after 16A were extraneous to the message. Now, having exhausted all other avenues of breaking the code, he gave the numbers a fresh look.

"Brian, why are the numbers different down here?" Olson asked. "You were diligent about not repeating pictures higher up, and all of a sudden, you are repeating several numbers."

Regan read the trinomes a few times before lifting his head up and staring blankly at Olson. He was no less puzzled than Olson was.

The brainstorming had lasted more than six hours. Neither Carr nor Olson felt they could go on any longer. Olson gave Regan a copy of the code and asked Regan to continue thinking about the numbers at the bottom when he went back to jail.

"Can I take the yearbook with me?" Regan asked. By this point, he seemed as keen as Olson and Carr to solve the puzzle he'd created three years earlier.

"Yes, you can take it back to your cell," Carr said. It was late in the afternoon when the U.S. marshals escorted Regan out of the courthouse and back to the Alexandria Detention Center.

On the weekend after the marathon meeting, Carr got a phone call from an Alexandria jail superintendent. "Mr. Regan wanted me to relay a message," the superintendent said. "He has completed the task that you assigned him."

Working with pencil and paper in the solitude of his cell, Regan had finally unlocked his memory of the encryption. He had focused on the trinomes at the bottom of the sheet, as Olson had suggested. At some point, the solution had bubbled up from the caverns of his subconscious.

When Carr met him at the courthouse the next day, Regan told him how it worked. Those anomalous trinomes at the bottom— there were twenty-four in all—weren't garbage.

They were coordinates. Hidden in plain sight.

Masked by the lines that came before them, the trinomes were Regan's "back door." Just as he'd done while encrypting the Virginia coordinates, he'd made sure to build a safety hatch for himself, knowing that he could forget how the code worked. What he hadn't anticipated was that the very existence of the back door could fade from his memory, defeating its purpose. Without Olson's prompting, he might never have remembered.

But now it had all come back to him, he explained to Carr.

The first two trinomes in the series—141 and 249—were the decimal digits for the latitude of the tree he had used as a reference for the first package. The next two trinomes—453 and 062—were the decimal digits for the longitude. As with the code for the Virginia packages, Regan hadn't bothered to write out the integer part of the coordinates—the numbers left of the decimal point, which were the same for the entire park: 39° north, 76° east. Combining these with the decimal digits provided the latitude and longitude for the first tree:

39.141249°N, −76.453062°E

The remaining twenty trinomes in the series, when broken up into sets of four trinomes each, constituted the decimal portion of the coordinates for five other trees. Although there were seven packages, there were only six tree references—Regan had used one of them as a marker for two packages. Regan had chosen three different areas of the park; at each of these areas, he'd buried two or three packages in fairly close proximity. As a result, the coordinates for the two trees he'd used as his markers in each area were identical up to the third or the fourth decimal digit. That explained why several of the trinomes at the bottom appeared twice in the series.

After figuring out the back door, Regan had also been able to recall all the steps for decrypting the trinomes in the first ten lines of the code. He explained them to Carr. The first step involved doing exactly what Olson had deduced in the brainstorming session: counting forward from Regan's picture to the portrait occupying the position given by the first two digits of the trinome. The next step was to add up the number of letters in that student's first name, or, if the student had a middle name, both first and middle names. This number and the third digit of the trinome had to be looked up on a simple 10-by-10 chart to resolve the trinome into the digit that it encrypted. The chart, which Regan had added as a second layer of encryption, looked like this:

```
1 2 3 4 5 6 7 8 9 0
2 3 4 5 6 7 8 9 0 1
3 4 5 6 7 8 9 0 1 2
4 5 6 7 8 9 0 1 2 3
5 6 7 8 9 0 1 2 3 4
6 7 8 9 0 1 2 3 4 5
7 8 9 0 1 2 3 4 5 6
8 9 0 1 2 3 4 5 6 7
9 0 1 2 3 4 5 6 7 8
0 1 2 3 4 5 6 7 8 9
```

Regan walked Carr through the steps with examples from the encrypted text. For instance, to decrypt the first trinome of the message, 146, one first looks up the fourteenth picture from Regan. Counting up the letters in the first name of that student, Sharon, gives the number 6. The trinome is now reduced to a two-digit number: 66. Next, one has to find the first digit of this number, 6, in the first column of the chart, and then locate in that row the second digit, which also happens to be 6. Then one has to go up to the top of the column in which the second digit has been found. The digit sitting at the top of that column—that is, in the first row—is the trinome's decrypt. In this example, that digit happens to be 1.

Similarly, the second trinome—051—leads to a picture of Patricia, with eight letters in the name. Going down to the eighth row of the chart, looking up the last digit of the trinome—1—in that row, and going up to the top of that column, one gets the decrypt: 4.

Not surprisingly, the first six trinomes resolve to 141249, and the next six translate to 453062: exactly the same as the first four trinomes at the bottom of the message: 141 249 453 062.

Regan gave Carr the results of his decryption. The encoded lines contained more than just the coordinates of the trees and the package descriptions, which Olson and Regan had worked out earlier. Along with the shortened latitude and longitude for each tree were two other pieces of information that would lead to the package. The first was the distance, in feet, one was supposed to walk from the tree. The second was a set of coordinates—once again abbreviated—that Regan had recorded at the location of the package.

Leaving the courthouse, Carr called Olson to relay how the code worked so that Olson could break out the message independently and validate the decryption Regan had provided. With the coordinates in hand, however, Carr didn't want to wait another moment to begin the search. "We're going out to look for the packages right now," he told Olson.

It should have been a snap to find the packages. Carr had anticipated that the mission would be accomplished within a few hours, maybe in a couple of days at the most. The last thing he had thought he would need to do was rent a backhoe.

Yet here he was, watching a rented backhoe being unloaded from a trailer at a parking lot inside the Patapsco Valley State Park. It was seven in the morning on April 22, several days after Regan had given Carr the decrypt of the coded message. Over the course of those days, Carr and his fellow agents had succeeded in finding all but one of the six trees that Regan had marked with roofing nails. The coordinates for each tree were precise enough to get to the tree's vicinity; scanning the area with metal detectors, the agents had been able to locate the exact tree. Some of the nails were barely visible on the trunk, having been obscured by new layers of bark that had grown in the years since Regan had been there.

Puzzlingly, though, none of the packages had been found. Carr and his colleagues had gone about the search exactly as they had in Virginia. From each tree, they had gone the specified number of feet on the side of the trunk opposite to the nail and dug. But despite digging large holes at those spots—deeper than the ones they had had to dig in Virginia—they had found nothing. The abbreviated coordinates that Regan had recorded for the package locations had not helped either. The limited precision of GPS in a forest, where signals from overhead geopositioning satellites tend to bounce off tree limbs and leaves while traveling through the canopy, meant an uncertainty of twenty meters or more in determining a particular site on the ground. At some of the locations, the reception was so poor that the agents struggled to get a GPS reading at all. The heavy foliage of spring didn't help the signals either. There was a reason Regan had needed to use the roofing nails as markers.

That's why Carr had requisitioned the backhoe. He and the other members of the search team stood by as it was taken off the trailer. One of the agents climbed into the driver's seat and drove it cautiously into the woods, to within a few yards of a nailed tree. Lowering the backhoe's giant yellow arm, he began scooping out large chunks of dirt. By noon, the excavation had turned the ground around the tree into a shallow crater.

There was still no sign of a package. The agents got out and dug further, turning the loose soil over with shovels to inspect every square inch with care. Still nothing.

The scene was to play out over and over through the next several weeks as the search continued fruitlessly. Carr remarked wryly to his fellow agents that some of the holes they were digging were big enough to swallow a Lincoln Continental. Speculating that Regan may have transposed the digits for some of the coordinates as he'd done for the twelfth Virginia package, the agents dug not only around the trees but also dozens of yards afield. At the end of each day's digging, the searched areas were pockmarked terrain, looking, in Marc Reeser's words, "like a Civil War zone where bombs had gone off." On the rare occasion that a jogger or horseback rider stopped by to ask what was going on, Carr had a cover story ready: the purpose of the excavation was to find the footprint of an old estate. A passerby called the state park office and inquired, in earnest, if a Walmart was being built in the park.

Unproductive as they were, the searches weren't entirely uneventful. In one instance, the backhoe toppled on its side while being driven across an especially uneven incline, and the agents had to use chains and all their strength to haul it back up. When a few attorneys from the Justice Department decided to join the search for a day, hoping to enjoy some time out of their offices, one of them lost his balance while stepping over rocks to get across a creek. The water was less than a foot deep, but enough for him to get soaking wet. The others struggled not to laugh.

Carr went back to Regan for pointers to focus the search but didn't learn anything useful. Somebody suggested hypnotizing Regan to get him to recall precisely where the packages were buried. Although the scientific support for using hypnosis to recover memories was weak, the FBI decided it was worth a shot.

A forensic psychologist named Michael Gelles was brought in for the job. He put Regan in a reclining chair in a corner of the debriefing room at the courthouse and dimmed the lights. Carr and another agent sat in another corner, watching the session in silence.

"I want you to focus on your toes, Brian," Gelles began soothingly. "Relax your toes." He went on. "Now focus on your calves. Relax your calves." Step by step, he directed Regan's attention upward, until he'd covered the whole body. If Gelles's suggestions had the hypnotic power they were supposed to have, Regan was by this point awash in calmness from head to toe.

"How are you feeling, Brian?" he asked.

"Relaxed," Regan replied.

"Let's take you back to when you were burying these packages," Gelles said. "Tell us, Brian . . ."

"Can I get up?" Regan asked, interrupting. He felt he could think better on his feet.

"Sure," Gelles said.

He proceeded to ask Regan questions about the three areas in Patapsco that he'd buried the packages in. From the corner of the room, Carr listened intently to Regan's responses and took notes. It wasn't clear from the answers if Regan was truly tapping into hitherto inaccessible memories of his activities from three years earlier or if he was merely playing along.

Much of what Regan recounted was too vague to be of value, although he did have a few specific descriptions. At one of the sites, he said, he'd come across a fallen log shaped like a Y: he recalled having buried a package just to the left of where the log bifurcated into the two prongs. At another site, near one of the marked trees, Carr's team had found an old tire. Regan remembered the tire: he told Gelles that he'd buried a package to the right of it.

Vivid as these recollections were, they didn't help the search. While Carr and his fellow agents didn't mind that they were spending their workdays tramping through the woods rather than being at their desks, there was a mounting sense of frustration. The digging was getting tiresome. Carr could see no end point in sight. There was just one thing left to do, he told Jechorek: get Brian Regan out of jail to the state park to see if he could just show them the sites.

On a cold and rainy morning in late May, Brian Regan stepped out of the back of an SUV near McKeldin Rapids at the north end of Patapsco Valley State Park. His wrists were handcuffed in front of him, hidden under a green rain poncho that covered him down to the waist. Worried that Regan's prison uniform might invite needless attention from hikers, Carr had made him change into a T-shirt and a pair of maroon sweatpants before they left the jail. Days earlier, a fellow inmate had given him an unflattering haircut, using a razor to shave a band around his head. As Regan entered the woods with Carr and his fellow agents, half a dozen SWAT team members fanned out in the vicinity, watching his every move.

Carr had not had an easy time selling Jechorek on the idea of bringing Regan out of prison. When she finally agreed, she had insisted on a comprehensive written plan to guarantee that Regan wouldn't escape or hurt himself. That meant having a paramedic on hand and mapping the shortest route to the nearest hospital from different parts of the park. The jail authorities had driven home the responsibility Carr was taking on when he checked Regan out. "If you lose him, don't come back," he had been told, not quite in jest. As the group made its way to the first site, walking along a stretch of forest that lay between a cliff and the Patapsco River, Carr had a momentary bout of anxiety thinking about the prospect of Regan breaking into a run and flinging himself over the cliff. He was reassured to see a SWAT team member walking along Regan's left, perfectly positioned to stop Regan from attempting a jump.

There was nothing in Regan's behavior to suggest that he might do something dangerous or unexpected, and everybody was more relaxed by the time they got to the first location. Regan surveyed the trees around him. Many of them had an orange ring painted on the trunk to indicate that they had been scanned for nails. Carr pointed out one on which nails had been found.

Walking a few paces from the tree, Regan came to the Y-shaped log that he'd mentioned in the hypnosis session. He straddled the top of the log, with one foot inside the Y and the other foot outside, and fixed his gaze at the reference tree. Then he bent forward, lowering his head, and looked at the tree again, squinting.

"I buried it there," he said matter-of-factly, moving his cuffed hands under the poncho to point at a spot a couple of feet away.

Carr had expected that Regan would need a measuring tape to determine how far away from the tree the package might be. Instead, Regan was relying on his visual memory. Carr was skeptical.

"Brian, I can't remember which tree I peed on two months ago," he said. "And you're telling me you buried a package here three years ago."

Reeser grabbed a shovel and began to dig. The earth, softened by the rain from earlier that morning, offered little resistance. He scooped up the dirt and tossed it to the side, an action that he and the other agents had mastered over the past few weeks. Regan looked on, his face betraying no emotion.

Minutes later, after Reeser had dug about a foot and a half, his shovel made a hard sound announcing contact with something solid. Breathing heavily, Reeser reached over and pulled the object out of the dirt. It was a package the size of a school lunch box, wrapped tightly in plastic.

Reeser took a knife and cut through the wrapping. Inside the package were a number of disks marked "Top Secret." They contained the *Joint Tactical Exploitation of National Systems* manual— the guidebook to the U.S. military's satellite and signals intelligence capabilities.

Reeser showed the disks to Carr, who looked at them, momentarily stunned. What they had just dug up was one of the country's most prized secrets, describing in detail America's vast and hidden network of reconnaissance systems and providing the U.S. war fighter with guidance on how to take advantage of those systems. To have even a few pages of this manual end up in the hands of an adversary would seriously compromise U.S. intelligence gathering. To have a foreign spy service acquire the entire *JTENS* manual—that, too, in digital form—would have been an intelligence disaster on an unparalleled scale, potentially undermining the U.S. military for decades. If the agents needed a concrete symbol of what the stakes had been in the two-year pursuit of Regan, those disks would have served the purpose.

With the first package unearthed, Carr felt a huge sense of relief. The agents led Regan on through the forest to the second of the two locations he had chosen in that part of the park. Here, too, Regan was able to remember where he'd buried the package. He also recalled now, he told Carr, that for many of the packages, he'd measured the distance of the package not from the tree marked with the nail, as had been assumed, but rather from a second tree that stood directly across from the first, in the direction that the nail pointed at. He had created the offset to add a second layer of security to his hiding scheme, once again not realizing that he could forget this important detail. As Carr and the others would find out, Regan's execution of the scheme, too, had been far less than perfect. In some instances, he had failed to point the nail in the right direction, which made it a challenge to identify the second tree correctly.

Sitting down at a picnic table, the agents opened the second package and found a handful of VHS tapes. In them, Regan had copied the contents of classified training videos checked out from the library he once maintained for his division at the NRO. When the agents unfolded the package wrapping, they discovered in one of the inner layers a yellow Post-it note that had Regan's name and extension number on it. Despite all of the meticulous planning to remain untraceable, he had left behind what Carr would later refer to, in the driest of understatements, as a "clue."

Reeser couldn't resist joking about it then and there.

"Brian, you left a sticky in here with your name on it," he remarked.

"I did?" Regan asked, his tone flat as usual.

"Yeah," Reeser said, chuckling. "The only thing missing from the note was a 'Please Return To.'"

Two weeks later, on June 11, the FBI brought Regan out to Patapsco a second time. Reeser, curious to know more about Regan's life, sat with him in the back of the SUV. Carr sat in the front, in the passenger seat. Unlike Reeser, he wasn't keen to chitchat with

Regan, even though he was impressed by and grateful for Regan's savant-like visual memory. Despite reaching the end of the investigation, he couldn't help feeling angry toward Regan for what the former master sergeant had done.

The SUV left the prison and headed for the state park, the SWAT team following in a second vehicle. Initially unresponsive to Reeser's attempts at getting to know him, Regan eventually opened up enough to give Reeser a brief glimpse into his life and the circumstances that had led him to plot espionage. His mounting burden of debt and the stress of raising four kids on a single modest income in one of the most expensive metropolitan areas of the country—compounded by the misery of an eighty-mile commute to work and back every day—had put him over the edge, he explained. He simply needed the money.

The vehicles entered Patapsco and parked in a meadow. Regan had buried two packages in the nearby area—one in a low-lying glade and the other on a neighboring hillside. The group walked to the lower site, which was lush with tall grass. Regan, wearing a blue Windbreaker that belonged to Carr, squinted in the bright midmorning sun. There weren't many landmarks in the clearing where the package was supposed to be, and he struggled to recall where he'd dug in relation to the marked tree in the vicinity. He was confused about which tree he'd measured the distance from; he wasn't certain if he had, in fact, used the double-tree system for this package. He provided his best guess, and the agents dug down a couple of feet there but couldn't find anything. Seeing how soft the soil was at this site reminded Regan that he'd buried the package deeper in the ground. Carr was confident that they'd find the package with some more digging and decided that they could return to it later.

The agents took Regan to the hillside, making their way up through some dense woods. It would have been hard for Regan to keep his balance walking uphill with his wrists handcuffed together, and so Carr freed Regan's left hand and cuffed the other to a belly chain around his waist. The sun was getting hotter, the air more humid. When they'd climbed up to the site, everybody took a moment to catch their breath.

Regan looked around at the trees on the slope.

"OK, now, let's recap what we have here," Carr said, leaning against a tree as he spoke. He went over some of the details that Regan had shared during the debriefings.

"You climbed up, you were out of breath, you laid your tarp out, you were digging," Carr said. Regan had described bringing a tarpaulin sheet with him to pack up any dirt left over after burying a package.

Regan nodded, still catching his breath.

"You remember there was some slope, right?" Carr asked. "Because the dirt was sliding off your tarp, correct?"

Regan nodded again, vigorously. He remembered this quite well.

Carr began walking from the tree he was leaning on. Regan followed him, treading over dry leaves that layered the ground. "This is the slope right here," he said, when they'd walked a few paces.

"The nails are right here," Reeser said, standing higher up by the reference tree.

"Yeah," Regan said, continuing to walk farther down. "The dirt was rolling downhill." He motioned with his free hand to show the slide.

"This looks about the slope you were working off?" Carr asked.

"Yeah," Regan said, looking up.

"What was the distance here, Marc?" Carr asked, wanting to know the number of feet Regan had put down for this package.

"Six feet," Reeser replied.

Regan looked up at the marked tree and the one across from it, taking a moment to estimate where that distance would be, if measured from the second tree, as he recalled having done.

"That would put you back here," he told Carr, pointing at the ground a couple of feet from where he stood. With his foot, he removed the leaves from the spot.

A SWAT team member named R. J. Porath who had been watching impatiently grabbed a shovel and started digging. Shortly after, Reeser, looking into the expanding hole, caught sight of the package.

"That's it," Reeser said.

"Look what you did, Brian," Carr said, admiringly.

Regan gave a nod of acknowledgment while Porath continued digging the dirt out around the package.

"Does this help with any of the other sites?" an agent asked.

"Oh yeah," Carr replied. "This validates the theory of the second tree."

Porath pulled the package out and heaved it onto the side. It was a large Rubbermaid container stuffed with documents.

"Look familiar?" Reeser asked, turning to Regan, who stood next to a tree, his hand resting on the trunk.

Regan nodded, looking downcast. For the first time, his characteristic neutral expression seemed to have been replaced by a profound sadness.

"Is there going to be just one there?" somebody asked.

Regan nodded again, with pursed lips.

It was past noon. As had been the case on their last excursion, Carr was under strict instructions from the jail authorities to bring

Regan back to prison at the earliest. The agents hiked down the hill to the meadow where the SUVs were parked. The group exited the park and stopped for lunch at a McDonald's.

"I got this, Brian," Carr said.

His offer to buy Regan's meal evoked a chuckle from Reeser, who found it comical that Carr had so magnanimously stated the obvious. After all, Regan—sitting in handcuffs—was clearly in no position to pay.

"Big spender, huh?" Reeser joked. Carr knew he was going to be teased about it for years to come. He turned to look at Regan.

"What do you want?" he asked.

"I want a quarter pounder with cheese, with no onions," Regan said. "I want mustard on it. No mayo." He was about to add more detail to the order when Reeser interrupted him.

"Brian, this is not a five-star restaurant," Reeser said. "Why don't you just get a quarter pounder and be done with it?"

"Well, I don't get it that often," Regan replied. "So I want to get what I want."

Carr and Reeser went into the restaurant, asking a couple of SWAT team members to stay with Regan in the vehicle. Carr returned with a cheeseburger for Regan, which he chowed down in a few quick bites. With encouragement from the SWAT team members, who suggested he take advantage of the opportunity, Regan ended up eating a couple more burgers. Not long after, Carr handed him over to the guards at the Alexandria jail, where he changed into his prison clothes before being escorted back to his cell. This was not the life he had imagined.

Brian Regan was a pioneer, the first spy to exploit digital access to American defense secrets on a massive scale. His actions of pilfering classified information from the intelligence community's servers foreshadowed the handiwork of Edward Snowden, the NSA contractor who downloaded hundreds of thousands of files from the Department of Defense and the NSA, and U.S. Army private Chelsea (Bradley) Manning, who lip-synched to Lady Gaga while exfiltrating more than seven hundred thousand pages of classified and sensitive information stored on government computers. If the intelligence community had done a better job of understanding the vulnerabilities laid bare by Regan's theft, and applied those lessons to fortify its digital networks from insider threats, the devastating leaks by Snowden and Manning—driven though they were by supposedly nobler motivations than Regan's—could have been prevented. (Whether it would have been desirable to prevent Snowden and Manning from making the disclosures is a different debate.)

This is not to say that the NRO and the FBI didn't delve deeper into Regan's crime after all the buried secrets had been recovered. Through the end of the summer and the early fall of 2003, Carr and other investigators, including the NRO's Bob Rice, interviewed Regan over dozens of hours to learn precisely how he'd gone about planning and executing his espionage. The answers he provided in these debriefing sessions helped them fill in the details of the picture they had pieced together during the course of the investigation. He confirmed that he had meticulously studied espionage cases on Intelink to come up with what he hoped would be a foolproof plan. It was shocking for Rice and other NRO officials to hear Regan describe the ridiculous ease with which he was able to print and copy a vast number of classified documents. Even more embarrassing for the agency—which spends hundreds of millions every year on security—was Regan's account of how he'd walked out of the NRO building, day after day, with classified materials hidden in his gym bag. Somebody stealing books from a library could have been at greater risk of getting caught.

Regan explained how and why his plan had evolved over time. By the early spring of 2001, he had abandoned the hope that the Libyans would ever respond to his offer: that's why he never saw the ad the FBI had placed in the *Washington Post*'s classified section. When he traveled to Europe in June and failed to market himself despite meeting with the Libyans face-to-face, he decided that he needed to bring along a sample of recently collected U.S. intelligence in order to be taken seriously. He also visited a handful of Swiss banks on the June trip, hoping to get himself a locker in which to stash the proceeds. The banks told him that he would first need to open an account, which would require a significant deposit. Regan hoped that the Iraqi and Chinese intelligence officials he expected to make contact with in Europe on the next trip would give him enough money in cash for the sample information— the missile coordinates, the classified course descriptions—to help him open a Swiss bank account. In case he still had trouble getting a locker, he planned to hide the money, which explained why he packed a GPS and a shovel and packing tape for the trip that was prevented by the FBI.

For Regan to think that he wouldn't be viewed with suspicion when he walked into those embassies was naïve but understandable. There was a grain of truth in his defense lawyer's characterization of his scheme as a "spy fantasy." Unlike earlier traitors such as the CIA's Aldrich Ames and Jim Nicholson, whose experience in spying on behalf of the United States and liaising with foreign intelligence officials gave them the knowledge and cover needed to conduct nefarious transactions with the enemy, Regan had never had any occasion to gain firsthand experience with the spying business. He was a dilettante, teaching himself the tradecraft by relying on books and movies.

Even a lot of the cryptography Regan used was self-taught. He remembered very little from the basic cryptanalysis course he had taken early in his career. When Olson interviewed him about the codes after the packages had been dug up, Regan told him that his enciphering had been driven both by his concern for security and by his paranoia about forgetting the key, which had happened to him once when he encoded the name and number of an old girl-friend. He came up with the idea of using his yearbook for a key for the Maryland coordinates after he saw the movie *Manhunter*, in which Hannibal Lecter relies on a book code to communicate with the killer known as the Tooth Fairy. Months later, while encrypting the Virginia coordinates, he decided it was better to use a key that he could carry with him at all times without its looking suspicious—hence the choice of the three NRO phone lists. For somebody with only a rudimentary knowledge of cryptography, these steps toward improving security demonstrated remarkable creativity.

But in inventing encryption schemes of his own, he had made things too complex—not just for the FBI but also for himself. Olson pointed out to him that there was no need to have added the second layer of encryption he had—using those number tables—in both the Virginia and the Maryland codes.

"You could have accomplished the same thing by using a one-time pad," Olson said, referring to a well-known and relatively simple encryption technique involving a random key.

"What's a onetime pad?" Regan asked him, betraying his ignorance of cryptographic systems.

The deeper the investigators delved into Regan's treason, the more they were amazed by the mismatch between his outward persona and his inner self. Reading the dozens of handwritten notes found in Regan's car and house, Carr and his fellow agents could have been forgiven for viewing him as a clueless dope. They chuckled at his reminders to pack "moose" for his thinning hair before going on trips. It baffled them to see that he needed to write instructions for himself on how to commute to work. They joked about his confidence in his investment acumen, which they greatly doubted when they looked at his online stock trades and read his nuggets of financial wisdom, one being that he would put all his money into gold. "Brian's got another investment strategy," they joked. "Buy low, sell high."

Analyzing his plot, however, revealed a cunning and diabolical mind. Regan's idea of creating preloaded dead drops to be sold later, after a buyer had been found, was a brilliant one. Although it would seem obvious in hindsight, his exploitation of digital access to classified information was pioneering. Investigators had to concede that they might never have found the buried packages without his help.

Yet, despite the brilliance of his plan, Regan's propensity for blunders all but guaranteed his failure as a spy. At nearly every step in the execution, he tended to make some kind of last-minute error, inevitably and unerringly, similarly to how he couldn't avoid misspelling words. Despite knowing that spellings weren't his strong suit, he failed to correct them before sending out his offer to foreign intelligence services, which likely made him look like a potential liability to whoever's desk the offer landed on. When he rented the storage unit near Richmond to store the hidden documents, the false name he used for the rental was "Patrick Regan"—something that could have easily led investigators to him, had they stumbled upon it. Summing up this proclivity to be brilliant for part of the way and then take a sudden left turn to stupidity, Reeser named Regan "Mr. Eighty Percent."

Regan's flaws in execution might have been trivial compared to his errors in judgment. Where others might have gone to a financial counselor to find a way out of debt, or sought help from friends, he dreamed up the most risky solution imaginable. Once caught, he grossly miscalculated the leverage he had in his negotiations with the U.S. government: despite being faced with the death penalty, he deluded himself into thinking that he would be able to bargain his way out using the packages he had buried. As if that wasn't bad enough, he undermined his position further by involving Anette in a complex plan to cover up his crime, leaving her at risk of being prosecuted.

Together, these decisions amounted to nothing short of legal hara-kiri. They seem to have been the product of a person hell-bent on proving others wrong, no matter how devastating the cost to himself. If Regan's perverse bid for riches and respect was partly driven by society's underestimation of his intelligence, in the end, he appeared to have hammered the nails into his coffin by overestimating his intelligence.

In March 2008, interviewed by NRO officials in prison, Regan seemed to have gained the sort of clarity that is bestowed only by the passage of time. He said he had lost touch with reality when he began plotting treason and had talked himself into thinking, right up to the trial, that he wouldn't get convicted. Even though he didn't think he deserved life in prison, he admitted that he had sealed his fate by not accepting the plea agreement offered to him.

"If I had understood that the financial situation could be corrected somehow, I wouldn't have gone off the deep end," he said in another interview with the NRO a few years later. "I felt the only option I had was to sell something." He'd chosen countries in the Middle East, he explained, because they had "oil money" and weren't very sophisticated in their intelligence gathering. "My goal was never to bring harm to the United States. I didn't want anybody to get killed. I just needed the money. I thought I could get some cash to solve my problems." All his life, he had strived to escape his doltish image, but it had chased him like a shadow until the two had tragically become one.

ACKNOWLEDGMENTS

This book could not have been written without the generous co-operation of more than a dozen individuals from the U.S. intelligence community, most of all Steven Carr, the lead FBI agent for the Brian Regan espionage case. When I first interviewed Carr in 2009 for an article in *Wired* magazine, I did not know that he had beaten cancer a few years earlier. Steve wasn't one to draw attention to his triumphs. I might have never learned of his illness but for a relapse of his leukemia in the spring of 2011, when I was interviewing him again to write a proposal for this book. Steve got a bone marrow transplant and, over the next several months, made a miraculous recovery, which we celebrated with one of his favorite lunch dishes: a Greek salad at a restaurant in College Park. By the summer of 2013, when the book proposal was doing the rounds of publishing houses in New York, Steve had fully regained his health, and the cancer seemed like a distant memory.

Unfortunately that fall, on the very day that I called Steve to share the good news about having found a publisher, he told me that the leukemia was back. Sensing despair in my voice, he reassured me that he was going to fight it with all his strength. Knowing that death could be hovering in the near future, he began sitting down with me for interviews in between chemotherapy sessions. Although he was proud of having led the Regan investigation, I knew that he was accommodating me only because of his commitment to support me in writing the book.

My admiration for Steve grew over the next year as he continued his battle. He got a second bone marrow transplant and went into remission once again before the disease struck back at the end of 2014. He fought, a fourth time, with invincible hope and an iron will, undergoing cancer immunotherapy in Seattle. Through all of the struggles, he never lost his good humor, fortifying the spirits of his well-wishers with a string of jokes, delivered with a perfectly deadpan expression. Updating his friends from Seattle through the Web site CaringBridge, he wrote, in May 2015:

> As a Cancer patient, you get asked a lot of routine questions by medical folks on a regular basis. In my ten years of treatment, I have developed an entire repertoire of smart-assed responses. I do this to lighten the mood, and to build rapport because nurses treat pleasant patients better and because it is just the way I am. For instance, when asked my birth date for verification, I often respond "why you asking, you gonna send me a card?" When asked how much I am drinking each day my pat answer is "2 or 3 scotch and sodas each night" (a BIG no-no). When asked if I smoke—"I just started" I say, "up to three packs a day, now. How am I doin?" I won't share my responses to the question—How's your poop?—but I have numerous depending on the crowd.

The immunotherapy did eliminate Steve's cancer, and he returned home in the middle of the summer in 2015. Days later, he was back in the hospital fighting an infection. Any other person would have had no time for a reporter in such circumstances, but Steve answered my questions from his hospital bed at Johns Hopkins.

"You'll be better soon, and we'll go get a Greek salad from that restaurant in College Park," I said before leaving.

"Heck, we'll just make one at home," he answered.

The only condition that Steve had laid down for the project was that the book give appropriate credit to his colleagues at the FBI who had worked on the case. A significant contributor to the investigation was the cryptanalyst Daniel Olson, to whom I am especially indebted for patiently explaining and reexplaining Regan's complex codes to me. The person who facilitated these interviews for me at the FBI Lab in Quantico was Special Agent Ann Todd: she deserves a big thank-you, not just because she set up those conversations with Dan but more so because she was the one who first drew my attention to the Regan case. I owe a big debt of gratitude to many others at the FBI who collaborated with Steve Carr on the investigation, and subsequently granted me dozens of hours of their time to share their recollections of the case: Lydia Jechorek, Bill Lace, Kathy Springstead, and Marc Reeser. These interviews would not have been possible without the support of the FBI's public affairs specialists—beginning with Betsy Glick, Beth Lefebvre, and Susan McKee at FBI headquarters, as well as Perryn Collier at FBI Phoenix and Amy Thoreson and Richard Wolf at FBI Baltimore.

The book has also benefited immensely from the help of Joshua Stueve, public affairs officer at the U.S. Attorney's Office for the

Eastern District of Virginia, who helped me sit down for interviews
with one of the nation's top national security prosecutors, James
P. Gillis. I also couldn't have done without the cooperation of Gary
Walker and Bret Padres, both of whom were part of the Regan
investigation, and the interviews provided by Michael Rochford,
former head of the espionage section in the FBI's counterintelligence division, as well as former FBI special agent Tom Reilly. I'm
grateful also to Keith Hall and Marty Faga—former directors of
the National Reconnaissance Office (NRO)—and Major General
Robert Rosenberg, a veteran of the national security space program,
for educating me about the history of the NRO. I am indebted as
well to David Kahn, author of the classic *The Codebreakers*, for
his generous advice on researching the history of cryptology and
ciphers.

I might never have thought it feasible to delve into Brian Regan's
character—and, consequently, write this book—had it not been for
the help of David Charney, a forensic psychiatrist who was hired by
Regan's defense team. Charney's insights into Regan's psychology
and motivations—derived from his many hours of interviews with
Regan—were key to my research into what shaped Regan's personality and what drove him to plot espionage. I'm thankful also to the
handful of friends, acquaintances, and colleagues of Regan—some
named in this book—for helping me understand him. I am especially
grateful to Michael Gould, Bob Florio, Cliff Wagner, and Peter
Klopfer, who helped me learn about Regan's growing-up years.

The book would not have seen the light of day but for the editors
at Penguin who believed in the story, starting with Charlie Conrad,
who acquired the book, and followed by Brent Howard, who edited
it. Brent's deft touch and enthusiastic support were invaluable assets
that many authors can only dream of. I'm thankful, in equal

measure, to my agent, Lydia Wills, whose insightful comments helped to shape the proposal into a viable book. A special note of thanks, also, to Nicholas Thompson, my former editor at *Wired*, who edited the January 2010 piece in the magazine that became the seed for this project.

I'm also indebted to the Wilson Center, the nonpartisan think tank that supported me with a five-month public policy fellowship in 2015. Having an office at the center to work at, and having the opportunity to interact with its talented pool of staff and scholars, was invaluable to me. I also benefited greatly from the research assistance I got from Hannah Armenta, my intern at the Wilson Center, who transcribed several hours of audio interviews.

Writing one's first book is a nerve-racking experience, and I wouldn't have been able to go through it without the help of my wife, Jen. A managing editor at *Aviation Week*, Jen spent countless hours listening to me talk about the story. Her feedback saved me time and again from taking a wrong direction in structuring the narrative. I could not have written the book without her support.

On September 11, 2015, after Steve had come back home from the hospital, I went to interview him again for the final chapters of the book. Even with an oxygen tank, he was having trouble breathing. His lung infection was proving to be stubborn. I told him I could come back another day, but he waved me into the house and had me turn up the oxygen flow so that he could answer my questions. After we'd gone for about two hours, I got up to leave. He smiled when I offered to bring him a Greek salad on my next visit.

It was the last time I saw him. Ten days later, he decided to go into hospice care, and he passed away—cancer-free—on September 25, 2015, at the age of fifty-three. At his funeral service, one of his friends read out a message that a fellow leukemia patient had posted on Steve's CaringBridge site.

Six years ago, right about this time of year, an FBI agent, a complete stranger, appeared in my hospital room at Johns Hopkins. I had just begun chemotherapy for A.L.L. Steve made periodic visits to that floor and asked the nurses if any newly diagnosed people had come in. He told me not to lose heart, that there was more living to do, that remission would give me time to know my kids, to live the kind of life you very often only learn you want to live when you're next to death. His buoyancy and gentle toughness were stalwart examples to me; he taught me how to do what I didn't think was possible. Steve and I relapsed at roughly the same time and spent many days together having conversations that we really couldn't have but with each other. He called me his brother in this illness and rarely have I been so proud. I learned so much from him about grace and kindness, about strength of character and holding on to hope. None of us knows how many days we have left. Not one of mine remaining will go by in which I won't think of him with love and admiration. See you on the other side, brother.

Thank you, Steve, for being the person that you were. If there is a heaven, you must surely be lounging there somewhere, enjoying a Greek salad.

A NOTE ON SOURCES

The material for this book has come from numerous sources: interviews with FBI agents and prosecutors and others involved in the investigation and trial of Brian Regan, court documents—including previously sealed documents that were unsealed by the court at the author's request—and a variety of government records obtained under the Freedom of Information Act. I've also had access to some of the notes and letters written by Regan while he was awaiting trial. My account of his growing-up years and adult life comes from multiple interviews with his friends, acquaintances, colleagues, and one family member, some of whom chose to speak on the condition of anonymity. The book has also benefited from my access to unclassified video recordings of the searches in Pocahontas and Patapsco.

Much of the dialogue in the book comes from the recollections of the individuals I interviewed. I've reproduced the recollected exchanges verbatim. The rest of the dialogue has been sourced from videos, letters, documents, and trial transcripts.

INDEX